THE SYMBOL OF THE SOUL
FROM HÖLDERLIN TO YEATS

THE SYMBOL OF THE SOUL
FROM HÖLDERLIN TO YEATS

A Study in Metonymy

SUZANNE NALBANTIAN

Columbia University Press
New York   1977

Published in Great Britain by The Macmillan Press Ltd.
Published in the United States by Columbia University Press

Printed in Great Britain

Library of Congress Cataloging in Publication Data

Nalbantian, Suzanne, 1950–
   The symbol of the soul from Hölderlin to Yeats.

   Originally presented as the author's thesis,
Columbia.
   Bibliography: p.
   Includes index.
   1. Poetry, Modern—19th century—History and
criticism.   2. Soul in literature.   I. Title.
PN1261.N3 1977   809'.933'53   76–25550
ISBN 0–231–04148–9

Contents

Preface

In the course of my doctoral studies in English and comparative literature at Columbia University I observed the changes in the philosophical
view of the soul reflected in the poetry of the nineteenth century. The
flexibility of the doctoral programme which I pursued made it possible
for me to encompass a diversified range of readings in poetry and philosophy.

I approached the problem of the soul through a variety of method-
ologies. In the first chapter I have treated my materials historically, in
the second to sixth chapters analytically; in the last two chapters I have
tried to reach a synthesis.

Throughout my research the guidance and encouragement of Professor Carl Woodring was most valuable to the progress of my work. I
am also very grateful to Professor Joseph Bauke who devotedly led me
through the comprehension of difficult German texts which I had found
essential to the composite viewing of my subject; and to Professor
James Mirollo whose orientation in comparative literature supported
wholeheartedly my scholarly objectives from one end to the other of my
doctoral studies. It is with utmost gratitude that I acknowledge the
Giles Whiting Dissertation Fellowship, which encouraged me to pursue
my objective uninterruptedly.

The translations from the French and German texts are my own, as I
approached all materials in the original language and offer them to
English readers in the spirit in which I read them. I wish others the
untranslatable pleasures of the original, and hope that an integrative
vision of the constellation of sensitive poets will be retained.

1 The Soul Concept as a Poetic Device

The word 'soul' has undergone endless philosophical speculations in the history of thought and has acquired a host of meanings and designations. The integrity of the term has been threatened by the related spiritual principles of mind and spirit. Both in philosophical discourses and in critical writings the notion of the soul has been obscure. *Anima*, the Latin word for soul, from which the French word *âme* is derived, originally designated the breath of life known in Greek as ψυχή. Of the four elements *air* was most closely linked with the soul on the basis of both its inherent constituent and the medium through which it travels. Like air, the soul is intangible and invisible, penetrates and cannot be delimited. *Anima* was distinguished from *animus* which stood for the mind.

Questions about the meaning of the soul have been the subject of repeated philosophical discourses of which the most early classic examples are Plato's *Phaedo* and Aristotle's *De Anima*. Platonic philosophy establishes a clear distinction between the divine soul and the mortal body. In looking for a Platonic definition of the soul, we find in Socrates' address to Cebes in the *Phaedo* the following typical position:

> Now, Cebes, he said, see whether this is our conclusion from all that we have said. The soul is most like that which is divine, immortal, intelligible, uniform, indissoluble, and ever self-consistent and invariable, whereas the body is most like that which is human, mortal, multiform, unintelligible, dissoluble, and never self-consistent.[1]

The soul, then, anxiously awaits its deliverance from the captivity of the body to attain its purified state in the realm of the Platonic absolute.

For a philosopher whose epistemology is most poignantly preserved in the renowned cave allegory in the seventh Book of the *Republic*, it is not surprising that equally revealing imagery illustrates the doctrine of immortality. The major metaphor around which the doctrine of immortality is construed is the prison. Aside from the various specific allusions to the body as prison-house, the entire dialogue can be read as an allegory in which the removal of the chains from the prisoner Socrates' feet and the final departure in death of the prisoner from the prison-house constitute the objectification of the soul's delivery from the mortal condition of the body. At a point in the dialogue where Socrates refers directly to the philosopher as a general practitioner of death and immortality through his daily contact with wisdom, we find a microcosm of the overall metaphoric pattern:

> Every seeker after wisdom knows that up to the time when philosophy takes it over his soul is a helpless prisoner, chained hand and foot in the body, compelled to view reality not directly but only through its prison bars, and wallowing in utter ignorance. And philosophy can see that the imprisonment is ingeniously effected by the prisoner's own active desire, which makes him first accessory to his own confinement. Well, philosophy takes over the soul in this condition and by gentle persuasion tries to set it free.[2]

The passage connects Platonic epistemology with ontology in a characteristic symbiosis of truth and immortality. Returning to the beginning of the *Phaedo*, we can recall that the work's nominal purpose is to describe Socrates' stoic acceptance of the death sentence. The place is the prison. The time is the morning of his death. Phaedo refers to the removal of the chains in preparation for the execution:

> The commissioners are taking off Socrates' chains, he said, and warning him that he is to die today.[3]

Socrates' reaction to an act which prepares for death is a feeling of relief:

> I had a pain in my leg from the fetter, and now I feel the pleasure coming that follows it.[4]

Interestingly, similar imagery is employed in the seventh Book of the *Republic* in which mortality is reflected in the picture of men bound by fetters and immortality in the ascent of the soul to the region of the sun. The whole structure of the *Phaedo*, however, most succinctly connects with the subject as the death of Socrates prompts the numerous arguments relating to the immortality of the soul.

Aristotle, like his Master, Plato, also makes an effort to 'determine what the soul is'.[5] His definition of the soul in *De Anima* conforms to his general division of existing entities into two components: matter (potency) and form (realization). Aristotle asserts that just as form realizes or actualizes the potential embodied in matter, so the soul is 'the form of a natural body which potentially has life.'[6] In Aristotle's view, then, soul and body coexist and are mutually interdependent: 'neither the soul nor certain parts of it, if it has parts, can be separated from the body.'[7]

Instead of the single word images of Plato, Aristotle appeals in the second Book of *De Anima* to two concrete analogies as illustrations of the abstract notion of the soul. The illustrations are drawn from the inorganic and the organic world: the axe and the eye. In both examples, the soul is analogous to the utilitarian function and actualization of the object. In the case of the axe, the soul is depicted in its ability to cut. In the case of the eye, the soul is the ability to see. In both instances, the soul imbues the object with vitality and acts as the active life principle.

Around the notion of the soul, Aristotle develops a psychology which specifies the various faculties of life by which the soul is defined in the hierarchy of living beings, ranging from nutrition to thought. It becomes readily apparent, then, that between these two philosophers' outright elaborations on the nature and function of the soul a major distinction emerges. Whereas Plato had conceived of the soul as an autonomous entity whose residence in the body was temporary until its liberation at the death of the body, Aristotle had envisaged the soul as form which was entirely dependent on and inseparable from body or matter. In Plato's discourses the soul was examined in an epistemological context. In Aristotle's treatise the soul was conceived as a topic of psychological discussion. The Greek heritage is therefore bifurcated concerning the nature of the soul. Where Plato refers to the soul in his search for true and complete identity of man and his eventual destiny, Aristotle is more concerned with the function of the soul in life situations.

Turning to the Christian framework, we can observe that the emphasis is upon the eventual destiny of the soul in the hereafter. Because of his stress on otherworldliness and his basic belief in the immortality of the soul, the Christian focuses on the transient nature of the soul in its earth-condition. Earth is an intermediate position between two eternal poles and the Christian is inevitably drawn to the notion of the *passage* of the soul on earth.

In classic examples of Christian doctrine drawn from the *Epistle to the Corinthians* – St Augustine, Pascal, Milton, to mention a few – attention is drawn either to the abode of the soul in its transitory condition or to its capacity to contain divine essence. In the sharp opposition of soul and body germane to Pauline doctrine, for example, we witness the readiness of the soul to shift from its temporary earthly residence to a permanent heavenly one:

> For we know that if our earthly house of this tabernacle were dissolved, we have a building of God, an house not made with hands, eternal in the heavens. For in this we groan, earnestly desiring to be clothed upon with our house which is from heaven. (II *Corinthians* 5 : 1–2)

At the same time, the soul, frequently designated as the temple, is the container of the divine God. The ambivalent function of the soul as the contained and the container receives poetic expression in a work such as

Milton's *Comus*, where the soul resides in the inner sanctum of the mind at the crossroads between the wordly and the divine.

If, as we know, Christianity emphasizes the temporary condition of the soul on earth and the dichotomy of soul and body, it is obvious that imagery relating to the soul will show the subservience of the body to the soul. For the Christian the body is the *means* by which the soul acquires its ultimate condition of immortality and is generally spoken of as the *instrument* of the latter. The functional value, then, of the body is highlighted. An illustration can be drawn from the following passage in St Augustine's *On Christian Doctrine*, in which the theologian instructs his followers into considering the body as a vehicle transporting the soul to God and returning it to its native country:

> Thus, in this mortal life, wandering from God, if we wish to return to our native country where we can be blessed we should use this world and not enjoy it, so that the invisible things of God being understood by the things that are made may be seen, that is, so that by means of corporal and temporal things we may comprehend the eternal and the spiritual.[8]

The basic metaphors illustrating Christian soul-concepts which can be culled from the works of a major popularizer of the Christian religion are important because of their large influence upon the major poets of the nineteenth century. The eighteenth-century illuminist Swedenborg, whose interpretation of Christian dogma became a widely accepted reference for the poets, provides a significant background for the metaphoric delineation of the soul.

Swedenborg inherits many of the traditional Christian metaphors regarding the soul's position on earth, such as the appellation of the soul as the dwelling place of God and the body as the instrument. But the probing character of his symbolic system and his fundamental concern with the problem of expressing the spiritual move him to focus on the tangible metaphors by which the soul manifests its immortality in the hereafter. The traditional Christian concern with the soul's journey on earth is envisaged in a secondary role as a correspondent of the soul's flight through the heavens.

In *Heaven and Hell* (1758) Swedenborg considers the knowledge of correspondences as a necessary prerequisite for the understanding of the meaning of the soul. He writes:

> Since, then, without a perception of what correspondence is there can be no clear knowledge of the spiritual world or of its inflow into the natural world, neither of what the spiritual is in its relation to the natural, nor any clear knowledge of the spirit of man, which is called the soul, and its operation into the body, neither of man's state after death, it is necessary to explain what correspondence is and the nature of it.[9]

Correspondences, which are the basis of Swedenborgian philosophy, establish a vital connection between the material world of the earth and the spiritual world realm of heaven. In stating that 'there is a correspondence of all things of heaven with all things of man'[10] Swedenborg lays the foundation for a metaphoric orientation. The conception of the soul as pure thought or vital principle is, according to Swedenborg, erroneous, for it defines the soul in earthly terms. Instead, Swedenborg designates the soul as pure spirit; although separated from the earthly body, which is its instrument during its sojourn on earth, the soul retains its human form in the heavenly realm.

A system of correspondence is set up where the body is most frequently construed as the clothing of the naked pristine soul not only in this world but in the hereafter as well. The entire physical machinery of the body and its sensory organs are assigned to the soul and receive spiritual significance. In particular, the senses of sight and hearing, the most spiritual of the five senses, are intensified. In terms of the soul, sight refers to inner sight or thought, hearing refers to inner hearing or perception. The rational faculty of man is nurtured by the heat and light of the sun, objective equivalents of Divine truth and love. The affections, or spiritual delights, are defined as communion with the Almighty. Imagery concerning cultivation is closely linked with the growth of the rational faculty as the seeds of knowledge are sown. Visual imagery prevails as the light of the Lord pervades the heavenly sphere and conveys the superior faculties that the soul obtains in its heavenly abode. For Swedenborg, the soul is a distinct presence which cannot be depicted in abstract terms and relies on concrete metaphors for an adequate explication.

With a different orientation from that of Swedenborg, the abstract notion of the *schöne Seele* developing in Germany in the eighteenth century should also be mentioned. Most evident in Schiller, this notion haunts the young German Romantics and is one of the connecting links between the German Classicists and Romantics. Associated with the soul is the *Sehnsucht* or infinite yearning for the absolute which is a major characteristic of German Idealism. Aesthetic and moral values are assigned to the soul in a characteristic eighteenth-century emphasis on humanity and the edification of man. The words *sehnen* and *ahnen* are among those most often linked to the soul in its striving away from the world of the senses (*Sinnlichkeit*) for the transcendent world beyond.

The classic instance of a soul caught between attraction to the earth and yearning for the Ideal is to be found in the following lines from Goethe's *Faust* in which the Promethean hero complains of two tendencies which beset him:

Zwei Seelen wohnen, ach! in meinen Brust,
Die eine will sich von der andern trennen;

Die eine hält, in derber Liebeslust,
Sich an die Welt mit klammernden Organen;
Die andre hebt gewaltsam sich vom Dust
Zu den Gefilden Hoher Ahnen. (I 1112–1117)[11]

Two souls, alas, dwell within my breast! the one would from the
other separate; the one, in earthy lusty love, does to the world adhere
with clinging limbs; the other rises mightily out from gloom to higher
intimations of fields above.

In effect, Faust gives up his soul when he becomes entirely content with
the life of the world and when he ceases to yearn for that perfection.
The frequent evocation of the soul in the German context at the time of
the writing of *Faust* shows how very present the notion of soul is in the
poet's consciousness. The focus of this study is not, however, on its
overall presence but rather on its poetic manifestation in imagery,
metaphor and metonymy.

As it is obvious in the above examples, each era's literary metaphor of
the soul reflects its religious and philosophical attitudes. Although views
and dogmas have altered from one era to another, the metaphor of the
soul conveys the distinct dichotomy that philosophers and poets have
sensed between man's physical and finite condition and his aspirations
for permanence and transcendence. What the various images have in
common, whether it be a soul delivered from the constraint of a prison,
a Psyche granted immortal status by the gods, a radiant unpolluted
shrine containing divine presence, an alien returning to his divine
household, or a perfected body whose faculties thrive by God's sustenance, is that they represent man's identification of that in him which he
deems permanent, designated as *soul*. When, however, we come to the
nineteenth century and scrutinize the imagery relating to the soul in the
course of a century, we find a mutation of metaphor that gradually
destroys that dichotomy and in so doing is suggestive of a basic change
in sensibility, ultimately leading to a state of spiritual shipwreck.

Where the early Romantic poets accept the metaphor of man's dual
existence as a basic element of their aesthetics, their followers become
increasingly distant from a spiritual orientation. The soul metaphor
changes gradually from an accepted theological reality to a stage in
which connections with theology are drastically severed. The metaphor
undergoes various phases in this process. At the beginning of the century
vestiges of previous soul metaphors are detected in the general metaphoric language used to invoke the soul and they become elements in
the effusive expression typical of the early Romantics. As the century
progresses a set of original, succinct, identifiable metaphors emerges and
reveals novel qualities that the soul acquires. Metaphoric complexes, to
borrow Gaston Bachelard's term,[12] are also developed. The strongest
coherence of symbol and significance is witnessed at a certain stage of

the evolution. With the waning of the century, there is the mutation of the soul metaphor into the cliché, a linguistic parallel to the erosion of the concept of the soul.

The poetic use of the signifier, soul, and the evolution of its significance, the focus of this study, is a striking phenomenon in the poetics of the nineteenth century. What is overwhelmingly apparent is the effect of the connotation of soul on poetic metaphor and the basic change in significance caused by the mutation of the original metaphor. The conduct of the concept in the medium of poetic language indicates important changes in the quality of poetic lyricism.

The vital connection between language and meaning was a major concern of the influential English critic I. A. Richards, who in *The Philosophy of Rhetoric* commented on the word as a unit of meaning:

> Most words, as they pass from context to context, change their meanings.[13]

In stressing the interdependence of words and context, he was inevitably led to a theory of metaphor which relied strongly on the interaction of its two components, the tenor and the vehicle, for its efficiency. The lowest level of metaphoric efficiency occurs, in his view, when the vehicle becomes mere embellishment. This is precisely what happens to the soul as it survives its significance in the form of cliché. There are, indeed, philosophical implications of the passage of the soul metaphor from early Romanticism to the Decadentism of the latter part of the century in English, American, French and German poetry, in fact throughout European literatures as well as in the allied arts.

Although the philosophical meaning serves as a point of departure and provides the background to the concept of soul, the language of the poetic writings harbouring the concept is the tangible evidence for the progress of the soul. Through the medium of poetic diction there is an implicit, unconscious, evolution in the meaning of the word. A *message* is conveyed by this process and if we turn to the external climate of the century, be it social, political or philosophical, it is merely to confirm what the lyric poet has unwittingly expressed.

The poet's language is the territory in which the soul concept reveals itself. Since this is a study in three languages, the words *soul, Seele* and *âme* are those by means of which we probe the soul concept. At one point, we shall be looking for the soul's position in the poem. At another point, we shall be watching it in action both as it draws certain word associations and as it activates a cluster of images. The general notions of the particular poets regarding the ego, the seat of sensitivity, the material world, the other-worldly vision, contribute as well to conclusions about the soul. An overall comparative camera which focuses on the movement of the concept develops the images and enables us to group patterns of soul into major trends and currents overriding national barriers.

Studies on the nature of the soul in specified literary texts are exceedingly sparse. Countless works have freely linked Romantic poetry with the soul. Often soul and imagination are interchangeable, and the soul is as easily identified with Romanticism as is the imagination. When C. M. Bowra, for instance, discusses the distinguishing characteristic of the spiritual in English Romantic poetry, he evokes the soul indiscriminately:

> The Romantic movement was a prodigious attempt to discover the world of the spirit through the unaided efforts of the solitary soul.[14]

Nor can one fail to mention Robert Langbaum's highlighted use of the word in an article entitled 'The Evolution of Soul in Wordsworth's Poetry'.[15] Langbaum associates the soul with the doctrine of experience which, as argued in his well-known book on the modern literary tradition,[16] is his characterization of Romanticism. In the particular article mentioned above, he says that in the case of Wordsworth, experience contributes to the evolution of the spiritual or the soul:

> And it is the main purport of Wordsworth's poetry to show the spiritual significance of this world, to show that we evolve a soul or identity through experience and that the very process of evolution is what we mean by soul.[17]

The French literary historian of Symbolism, Guy Michaud, speaking of the other end of the century, is equally aware of the predominance of the soul consciousness. He writes: 'L'âme c'est le mot-clé de l'époque.'[18]

In general, critical works tend to make passing reference to a certain image of the soul in a certain work and then proceed to discuss imagery of the mind or some related topic. This is true, for example, of M. H. Abrams' *The Mirror and the Lamp*.[19] In his section on the metaphors of the mind, Abrams makes several apt allusions to the imagery of the soul as a fountain in Romantic poetry but then directly proceeds to concern himself with the mind, which in the image of the lamp dominates his discussion of the expressive theory of art. The most notable study on the soul in the nineteenth century is Albert Béguin's valuable book entitled *L'Ame Romantique et la Rêve*. In this book, Béguin knits together early nineteenth-century Romantics with poets of the rest of the century through the word 'soul'. He views the soul and the dream as constants in the authors whom he studies ranging from Novalis, Lichtenberg, von Schubert, Tieck, Hoffmann to subsequent writers such as Hugo, Baudelaire, Rimbaud, Mallarmé and Proust. In discussing the general tendency toward analogy by the early Romantics, who conveyed a reciprocal relationship of man and nature. Béguin observes a resurgence of interest in the universal soul in their poetic works. He writes:

Avec la conception néo-platonicienne de l'animal-univers renaît l'idée d'une âme universelle omniprésente, principe spirituel de toutes choses, dont les âmes individuelles sont des émanations ou des aspects. Cette âme est la source d'où émanent à la fois la réalité spirituelle et le cosmos. Entre le plan transcendental des idées et le plan de la nature, il n'y a plus d'abîme, mais un lien commun. La nature est assimilée à une action inconsciente de cette âme qui devient consciente dans l'esprit humain, et qui est l'unité indivisible, considérée sous son aspect créateur.[20]

With the Neoplatonic conception of the living universe the idea of a universal omnipotent soul is reborn, a spiritual principle of all things, of which individual souls are emanations or aspects. This soul is the source from which spiritual reality and the cosmos emanate simultaneously. Between the transcendental plane of Ideas and the plane of nature, there is no longer an abyss but a common link. Nature is assimilated by an unconscious action of this soul which becomes conscious in the human mind, and which is the indivisible unity considered under its creative aspect.

Béguin is particularly drawn toward the soul as it projects inward to meet the divine in the dark landscape of the dream. However, in his enthusiasm over the dream world and the soul's participation in it, Béguin discusses the soul in philosophical and analytic terms and thereby fails to give concrete evidence of the conduct of the word 'soul' in poetic texts. He speaks of the shift away from the consideration of the soul as a centre of psyche. It becomes, rather, a metaphysical factor in the relationship between reality and ideal existence. Béguin distinguishes between earlier concepts of soul, centred on the function of the soul in the body and its relation to the mind, and the Romantic poets' focus on the alienation of the soul and its sense of exile on earth. He writes:

Le premier mythe fut celui de l'Ame: tandis que la raison décomposait l'être en facultés juxtaposées, rouages d'une machine démontable, une croyance inexpliquée, mais fervente, réaffirma l'existence d'un centre intérieur; principe de notre vie, lieu de nos certitudes, entité inaliénable, l'âme n'est plus l'objet de la curiosité psychologique, intéressée à déceler la fonctionnement de notre esprit. Elle devient une essence vivante, occupée de sa destinée éternelle davantage que de son méchanisme; elle sait qu'elle vient de plus loin ses origines connues et qu'un avenir lui est réservé dans d'autres espaces. Devant le monde où elle est venue habiter, elle éprouve l'étonnement d'une étrangère transportée parmi les peuples lointains. Une anxiété profonde la saisit, lorsqu'elle se demande jusqu'où s'étend son propre domaine: provisoirement exilée dans le temps, elle se rapelle ou bien elle pressent qu'elle n'appartient pas tout entière au monde de cet exil.[21]

The first myth was that of the Soul: while reason decomposed 'being' into juxtaposed faculties like an assemblage of wheels that can be disassembled, an unexplained but fervent belief reaffirmed the existence of an interior center; as a principle of our life, place of our certitudes, inalienable entity, the soul is no longer the object of psychological curiosity oriented toward disclosing the functioning of our mind. It becomes a living essence, concerned more with its eternal destiny than with its mechanism; it knows that it comes from further away than its known origins and that a future is reserved for it in other spaces. In the midst of a world which it has come to inhabit, it experiences the astonishment of a stranger transported amidst foreign people. A profound anxiety seizes it when it wonders how far its own domain extends: temporarily exiled in time, it remembers or else has intimations that it does not belong entirely to the world of this exile.

Béguin does not explain the application of this concept of soul in its functioning as a poetic device. What he does succeed in doing, however, is to characterize most persuasively the nineteenth century as the age of the soul.

Comparable to the thematic nature of Béguin's work are studies of such major critics as A. O. Lovejoy, Samuel Monk, Walter Silz, F. O. Matthiessen, M. H. Abrams, and Carl Woodring. They share a kinship in exploring a large body of literature and in discovering a unifying theme or aesthetic sensibility therein. As an historian of ideas, Lovejoy, for example, has given significance to the study of key concepts, words, ideas, which are current in a particular epoch and succinctly describe a general prevailing temper or spirit of an age. One of the elements of the critic's ideological quest is the following:

> Another part of his business, if he means to take cognizance of the genuinely operative factors in the larger movement of thought, is an inquiry which may be called philosophical semantics – a study of the sacred words and phrases of a period or a movement, with a view to a clearing up of their ambiguities, a listing of their various shades of meaning. . . .[22]

Lovejoy's own concentration on the unit-idea of the Great Chain of Being, needless to say, broke through national barriers and disciplines. Samuel Monk's *The Sublime*, using Lovejoy as a model, studies the aesthetics of the sublime in eighteenth-century England. Walter Silz, in his study *Early German Romanticism*, joins Romantic to Classic in considering broad lines of both movements and in viewing the Romantic movement in Germany as an evolution of German Classicism. In the field of American literature, we can turn to F. O. Matthiessen, who in the classic study *The American Renaissance* has tied together the bulk of nineteenth-century American literature by tracing major recurrent themes. For this critic diction and rhetoric were particularly revealing:

> An artist's use of language is the most sensitive index to cultural history, since a man can articulate only what he is, and what he has been made by the society of which he is a willing or unwilling part.[23]

Much of recent American literary criticism has focused on seminal poems replete with images and structures which serve to identify larger prevailing factors. This is true of M. H. Abrams' *Natural Supernaturalism*, which is concerned with the secularization of religious themes in Romantic poetry and Carl Woodring's *Politics in English Romantic Poetry* which points to the connection between basic ingredients of Romantic poetry and general 'human ideals of freedom, simplicity and humility'[24] current at the time. We see that a synthetic approach, characteristic of all these critical works, succeeds in crystallizing major tempers and moods of large eras.

As we will be concerned in our current study to group materials together from a variety of texts, we will see whether in so doing a possible system may well emerge to gauge the changing quality of poetic lyricism in the nineteenth century. Trends and transformations in the use of the word will be the basis of such groupings. Romantic poets such as Wordsworth, Hölderlin, Lamartine, Jean-Paul, Kleist, Novalis, Coleridge, Shelley, Keats, Poe, and Hugo are among the first to be considered. Distinctions will be sought within this body of poetry. We will see whether a major deviation in the Romantic definition of the soul does not particularly become evident as we proceed to examine the poetry of Baudelaire. Finally a radical shift in the nature of the soul will become apparent from the study of the concept in representative examples of Symbolist poetry, presaging the avant-garde.

Where the use of the word 'soul' is obvious and individual, we are not concerned. Since much of French Romantic poetry offers a static classical usage, it provides no interest to our developing line. In the same manner, the abundant use of the word 'soul' by the Pre-Raphaelites, with a predominantly Dantesque meaning, does not play a role in tracing the variable of the soul. In fine, the choice of poets to be used as a basis of discussion is occasioned by the frequency of the use of the word in their poetry demonstrating illuminating contrasts and development which can be perceived in the juxtaposition of representative examples of nineteenth-century poetic lyricism.

Once the individual mutations are studied, the codification of the various stages of the soul-concept will be possible. A synthesis will be attempted of the linguistic devices that convey the changing philosophy of which it is an expression. Where the gradual changes in the metaphor are in themselves interesting, the linguistic structures which evolve and the philosophical currents that emerge enable us to impose order on the plethora of examples gathered in our perusal through the lyric mode. There will be an attempt to classify the degrees of erosion of the Romantic soul as we study the apparent trend toward fragmentation and materialization of the soul-identity readily perceptible in the evolution of lyricism in the nineteenth century. The lyric poets will be grouped according to the degree by which their thought and expression reveal this shift in sensibility away from the world of the soul.

2 Wordsworth, Hölderlin and their Contemporaries: the Imperial Soul

In their frequent reference to the soul two early Romantic poets, Wordsworth and Hölderlin, demonstrate close affinities. Both born in 1770, they display in the years 1797–1807 poetic writings in which the soul is the focus of their sensibilities. Hölderlin completed *Hyperion* in 1799 and wrote versions of *Der Tod des Empedokles* between 1797 and 1800. The poems that pertain to this discussion, in particular those of an elegiac character, 'Menons Klagen um Diotima' and 'Brot und Wein' appear before 1807. Wordsworth's 'Tintern Abbey' appeared in 1798, followed by *The Prelude*, already conceived in its first version in 1805, and 'Ode: Intimations of Immortality from Recollections of Early Childhood', published in 1807. Within the ten years 'The Old Cumberland Beggar' and 'There is a Bondage Worse' were also written. This decade at the turn of the century is to be the first phase of our consideration of the metamorphosis of soul in the poetic language of the nineteenth century. For the most part, the word 'soul' is used ambiguously in the works of these two poets and figures most frequently in the context of elevation. The soul is evoked directly rather than indirectly in imagery. In the case of both poets the soul becomes the pivot around which earthly existence rotates, as the contemplation moves now inward, now outward. As the connecting link between pre-life and afterlife, the soul is the eternal constant in the earthly variables.

Wordsworth looms undeniably at the forefront of one of the larger strains in European Romanticism. The word 'soul' is in active poetic use in the period of Wordsworth's early writings from the time of the *Lyrical Ballads* in 1798, through the first version of *The Prelude*, to the 'Intimations' ode of 1807, before being set in a more orthodox Christian context in the later years of the poet. It takes neither the form of philosophical concept nor of poetic metaphor but rather is used loosely and ambiguously in the effusive language so characteristic of a poet who had defined his trade as the spontaneous overflow of powerful emotion. The use of this key word is significantly spontaneous and unpremeditated and incurs a meaning through the contexts in which it is set and the tone with which it is invoked. For a poet who had persistently protested against the ills of the material world and who had sought solace in nature to a point of seeming a near-recluse in his later years, it is not surprising that spiritual sustenance was of prime importance.

The most striking example of Wordsworth's perspective of the soul is in the well-known lines of his 'Intimations' ode:

Our birth is but a sleep and a forgetting:
The soul that rises with us, our life's Star,
  Hath had elsewhere its setting,
    And cometh from afar:
  Not in entire forgetfulness,
  And not in utter nakedness,
But trailing clouds of glory do we come
    From God, who is our home. (58–65)[1]

As a device for elevation and transcendence, then, the soul is revealed through its function rather than in distinct form. The vocabulary has a self-contained neo-Platonic doctrine. So, in Book VIII of *The Prelude*, for example, Wordsworth attributes to the soul 'prepossession', which is necessary for insight into the divine:

I had my face turned toward the truth, began
With an advantage furnished by that kind
Of prepossession, without which the soul
Receives no knowledge that can bring forth good,
No genuine insight ever comes to her. (VIII, 323–7)

The soul is man's contact with the 'sublime idea' of the Platonic absolute realm. If the wisdom of the soul is reminiscent of Platonic design, however, the majestic, ecstatic manner in which the soul's ascent to the region of God is pictured adds a Christian dimension to Wordsworth's representation of the soul:

    The soul when smitten thus
By a sublime idea, whencesoe'er
Vouchsafed for union or communion, feeds
On the pure bliss, and takes her rest with God. (VIII, 672–5)

Indeed, much has been written about the transcendent philosophy of the 'Intimations' ode and *The Prelude*, and there have been disputes as to the relative advantages of child versus man in the confrontation of the life-experience. It becomes apparent, however, that the condition of soul relates most closely to the pristine state of childhood, whereas that of the mind belongs to the mature state of philosopher, humanist. The most obvious instance of the conjunction of soul and child is in the passage from the 'Intimations' ode which designates the child as the container of the enormous soul and approaches the grotesque in the juxtaposition of the prodigious soul with the little boy:

> Thou, whose exterior semblance doth belie
>   Thy Soul's immensity. (108)

In fact, the *soul* takes on a dialectical position in relation to the *mind*. The power of recollection of the soul surpasses the power of the mind in its capacity to sense the intangible quality of divine presence. Wordsworth informs us that it is the soul, not the mind, that 'retains an obscure sense of possible sublimity' through the power of recollection:

> for I would walk alone,
> Under the quiet stars, and at that time
> Have felt whate'er there is of power in sound
> To breathe an elevated mood, by form
> Or image unprofaned; ...
> Thence did I drink the visionary power:
> And deem not profitless those fleeting moods
> Of shadowy exultation: not for this,
> That they are kindred to our purer mind
> And intellectual life; but that the soul,
> Remembering how she felt, but what she felt
> Remembering not, retains an obscure sense
> Of possible sublimity, whereto
> With growing faculties she doth aspire. (II, 302–6; 311–19)

A concrete instance of the type of experience which Wordsworth here describes in abstract general terms as 'possible sublimity' is to be found in the first book of *The Prelude* where he describes the encounter of his elfin pinnace with a huge mountain crag. In reviewing that sense of his childhood, he remembers the psychological effect of that experience:

> No familiar shapes
> Remained, no pleasant images of trees,
> Of sea or sky, no colours of green fields;
> But huge and mighty forms, that do not live
> Like living men, moved slowly through the mind
> By day, and were a trouble to my dreams. (I, 395–400)

Here is what Wordsworth calls in the subsequent passage, 'the passions that build up our human soul' (I, 407). It is the type of deep imageless truth which was to haunt Shelley in his appreciation of Mont Blanc. In Wordsworth's poetics, the contact with the sublime is offered specifically to the soul.

The word 'obscure' in the phrase 'an obscure sense of possible sublimity' is also particularly significant, for it stresses the undefinable quality of the visionary. There exists a balance in which what the soul loses of sublime vision, the mind replaces with 'tranquil restoration' and compassion for mortality.

Aside from the abstract language used to describe the soul's capacity of sublime vision, there is certain metaphoric language which is associated with the process. Imbued with the divine, the soul transcends the body. In such 'moments' man becomes pure spirit, divesting himself of all bodily attributes. The image of the veil becomes associated with this process. Take, for example, the following passage from the fourth book of *The Prelude* in which the poet recounts another moment of sublime vision which halts him as he saunters through the fields:

> Gently did my soul
> Put off her veil, and, self-transmuted, stood
> Naked, as in the presence of her God. (IV, 150–2)

Here the soul is described in its true and authentic state which is naked and pristine. The removal of frost is another metaphoric device used to convey the soul's capacity to dissolve time. The poet observes:

> How the immortal soul with God-like power
> Informs, creates, and thaws the deepest sleep
> That time can lay upon her. (IV, 166–8)

Removal of clothing and frost, that is, of covering and solidification, is at work in the process by which the soul recognizes itself and regains that eternity which is its birthright.

Covering is not only the suggestion of impediment to the soul's rise. There are also images implying weightiness. In the juxtaposition of the 'Intimations' ode and *The Prelude*, the struggle becomes obvious; there are the conflicting images on the one hand of the soul rising like a star following the path of rising and setting in pre-existence, and on the other hand of a soul grown heavy with earthly shackles. It would seem that the soaring represents the longing, or as the Germans might say, *Sehnsucht*, whereas the burdening suggests the gravitation toward earthly reality.

The most tangible metaphor which suggests the tension between the earthly condition of the soul and its ultimate capacity to transcend that temporary condition is the prison-house of the 'Intimations' ode:

> Heaven lies about us in our infancy!
> Shades of the prison-house begin to close
> Upon the growing Boy! (66–8)

Though restricted by the confines of the earth in its passage from infancy to adulthood, the soul has the inherent ability to return to its original condition of immortality. The temporality of its stay on earth is conveyed through the reference to man as the 'foster-child' of the earth. The alienation of the soul on earth is emphasized. The return of the native is conveyed in terms of the travel of the soul and the imminence of that process:

Our Souls have sight of that immortal sea
 Which brought us hither,
Can in a moment travel thither. (167-9)

The liberation of the soul from earthly chains simulates the instantaneous process of death. Finally, the voyage metaphor is sustained throughout the Ode, which conceives of the soul's journey from its original celestial home to the earth. There the soul abides for a span of time, then goes to its ultimate destination in God's 'imperial palace'.

Elsewhere there is reference to a fettered soul, particularly in the political poems which bemoan the loss of liberty. This is true, for example, in 'There is a Bondage Worse':

There is a bondage worse, far worse, to bear
Than his who breathes, by roof, and floor, and wall
Pent in, a Tyrant's solitary Thrall . . .
One of a nation who, henceforth, must wear
Their fetters in their souls.

Fetters are assigned to a nation which, in his view, has lost its ideals of liberty. We read of the bondage and enslavement of the soul in 'The Convention of Cintra'. In the course of decrying the 'selfish interest' which makes England sympathize with France in the war between France and Spain, the poet refers to the soul as the spirit of liberty being enslaved:

Not 'mid the World's vain objects that enslave
The free-born Soul – that World whose vaunted skill
In selfish interest perverts the will.

Only a return to Nature will restore that liberty and revive the soul. For the poet, the soul is captivated by the world which in the words of his famous sonnet is 'too much with us'.[2] Whether it be political tyranny, the material world, or the faculty of reason, it becomes clear that the soul struggles against those forces which attempt to subdue its most fundamental aspect of freedom.

When Wordsworth comes to revise *The Prelude* in his later years, he will make more use of the chain and fetter imagery in relation to the soul in the last book of the poem. In particular, he refers to the soul's communion with the heavenly and its freedom from chains through the power of the imagination:

Love that adores, but on the knees of prayer,
By heaven inspired; that frees from chains the soul. (XIV, 183-4)

Though this example occurs outside the decade we are examining, nonetheless we appeal to the imagery as characteristic and descriptive of the poet's concept of the soul revealed through language.

Above all, the buoyancy of the soul is exulted. Intermittently, in the

'Intimations' ode, Wordsworth shows how as the child matures there occurs a dimming of the vision of the soul and a corresponding worldly weight attributed to the soul incompatible with its natural character:

> Full soon thy Soul shall have her earthly freight,
> And custom lie upon thee with a weight,
> Heavy as frost, and deep almost as life! (130–2)

There is, however, no clear idea of the exact relationship of soul and mind in Wordsworth. An important passage from the second book of *The Prelude* demonstrates the characteristic confusion of the two terms. In referring to the imagination, the poet evokes both the soul and the mind:

> But let this
> Be not forgotten, that I still retained
> My first creative sensibility;
> That by the regular action of the world
> My *soul* was unsubdued. A plastic power
> Abode with me; a forming hand, at times
> Rebellious, acting in a devious mood;
> A local spirit of his own, at war
> With general tendency, but, for the most,
> Subservient strictly to external things
> With which it communed. An auxiliar light
> Came from my *mind*, which on the setting sun
> Bestowed new splendour. (II, 358–70)

In this passage, the soul is that first creative sensitivity, but the same can be said of the mind. In the first book we read 'fair seed-time had my soul' (I, 301), but we remember at the same time that *The Prelude* describes the 'growth of a poet's mind'. Though both positions point to the growth and nurture of the element of sensibility, the soul remains pristine and innate, where the mind is a faculty that develops. If the soul has the majestic divine right of royalty, the mind bears the venerability of a philosopher king.

The question of the exactness of the relationship of the soul and mind is not crucial to this study because Wordsworth is not a systematic philosopher but a philosopher-poet, and he works through words; among the most frequent of these are *soul* and *mind*, and the soundboard on which they sing in competition is *nature*. On the one hand it is through *soul* that Wordsworth finds direct communion with nature, on the other hand it is with *mind*; the contact with soul is in terms of something lost, the contact with mind suggests retrieving and holding on as in a receptacle. There is the search for something lost:

> Though nothing can bring back the hour
> Of splendour in the grass, of glory in the flower.

('Intimations' ode, 181–2)

There is the receptacle of what is retained:

> ... Thy mind
> Shall be a mansion for all lovely forms. ('Tintern Abbey', 139–40)

What does emerge from the body of Wordsworth's poetry is a concept of soul which transcends the particular allusions to the word in a given phrase or section of a poem. In the totality of Wordsworth's thought, the soul is an overall presence which looms imperiously and serves as the basis for the poet's fundamental spirituality.

It would seem that Wordsworth unconsciously conceived of the soul as an additional faculty granted in particular to the poetic mind. In Wordsworth's poetry, it is the *soul* which is engaged in endless commerce with the invisible world of the spirit; the visible world is used as the intermediary to the divine. The most fitting metaphor of the soul *would be* that of a tentacle which could, from the slightest sensation of exterior stimuli, sense an entire corresponding world. It is in this respect that we can interpret Wordsworth's all too frequent attention on what he calls 'mean objects' and humble things. The physical world of the common daffodil gives the poet's soul intimations of the higher world of the spirit in much the same way as the grain of sand offers an eternity to the older poet, Blake.

Perhaps the Conclusion to *The Prelude*, in its climactic section on Mount Snowdon, best conveys through its very language this overwhelming sense of soul. When Wordsworth, in this context, inspired by the immensity and height offered by the Alpine mountain of Wales, speaks of higher minds, he is in fact describing qualities inherent to the soul. They are roused and 'quickened' by outside stimuli. They receive impressions from the outside world and are able to manufacture from the 'least suggestions' the 'great things', that is, elements of the spiritual world. The quickening, arousal, and excitation are the particular movements attributed to the soul as it senses the approach of the divine. The entire movement charts a passage from the natural to the supernatural, from the human to the divine, from the earthly to the heavenly; and the soul is the powerful seat of these acts of transcendence.

In fact, the seat becomes a throne, and the human soul aspires to regain the majesty of its original state. In this light, we can identify the multiple designations of the soul in Wordsworth's poetry as the majestic, the imperial, the celestial, and the sublime. We have already noted the clearly defined progression of the soul in the 'Intimations' ode to its original state of immortality. In the closing lines of the seventh book of *The Prelude*, we witness the transition of the soul from the 'trivialities' of city life to the grandeur of the Nature scene which fosters its aspirations for majesty. The most characteristic posture of the soul is decidedly the majestic and its particular identifying trait is nobility. Before it, the universe lays bare its highest truths and hidden meanings.

As that pristine throne of sensibility, the soul is a godlike power which magnifies that which comes in its vicinity. It beholds, respires, projects, and communes with the eternal and universal. It experiences high 'delights' and 'transports' which serve to uplift the individual from the world in trancendent moments of bliss. In fine, for the poet, it is the active pulse, the under-agent, the immortal spirit of life, the centre of existence both at the core of mankind and at the centre of the universe, in the old Cumberland beggar, in the daffodil, in nature's manifestations, in the infant, in the poetic spirit: the 'living Presence'[3] at the core of 'every mode of being'.[4]

Like the philosopher-king Prospero of Shakespeare's *Tempest* who drowns his books and breaks his staff of artistry to return to a human- istic social world, the poet Wordsworth strays in later years away from that vitalistic, passionate sense of soul which was the major feature of his early poetic writings. In the ecclesiastical sonnets of the 1820s the sense of soul is no longer poetic and becomes, instead, woven into a traditional theological context. It is accordingly with that distinct *poetic* sense of soul of Wordsworth's early work that we proceed to observe manifestations of soul in other Romantic poets.

When we view Hölderlin in juxtaposition with Wordsworth, we note that the German poet makes no attempt to present a systematic pro- gression of the soul from earth to heaven as Wordsworth had in his 'Intimations' ode. Hölderlin's use of the word 'soul' is frequent and indiscriminate. The word appears whenever the qualities he wants to suggest do not fit into specific, concrete connotations or images. The meaning is abstract and is therefore rarely involved in metaphoric language at this stage of development. *Hyperion*, the principle work of Hölderlin relevant to our study of the soul, is composed of a series of letters in which the poet-hero relates the past experiences of his soul to a dear friend, Bellarmin. The individual human soul of the hermit Hyperion or that of the lyric poet is attracted toward the spirit of ancient Greece identified with the divine soul called Diotima. Her presence hovers over Hyperion and puts him in a state of ecstasy. She appears to touch the clouds and barely feels the earth beneath her feet. The contrasting images of 'Himmel' (heaven) and 'Erde' (earth) suggest her position in relation to Hyperion:

> Diotimas Auge öffnete sich weit, und leise, wie eine Knospe sich aufschliesst, schloss das liebe Gesichten vor den Lüften des Himmels sich auf, ward lauter Sprache und Seele, und, als begänne sie den Flug in die Wolken, stand sanft empor gestrekt die ganze Gestalt, in leichter Majestät, und berührte kaum mit den Füssen die Erde. (p. 57)[5]

> Diotima's eye opened wide, and gently as a bud opens up the little countenance appeared in the azure of the heavens, became pure

speech and soul, and as it began the flight in the clouds the entire form rose and spread forth serenely in light majesty, barely touching the earth with the feet.

The contact with the ideal is precarious because, as we learn in the course of the narration, Diotima dies and ancient Greece has been replaced by a modern one, divested of the glory and grandeur of its heritage. In the setting of Calaurea to which Hyperion sails, his imagination recreates the image of Diotima with whom he is able to have a soul-mate relationship. The love idyll occurs in an idealized Greece.

Although the same dichotomy exists between earthly and eternal existence as in Wordsworth, and the soul is the pawn between the two, in Hölderlin the struggle appears less patient, the soul more captive and more impelled by a force beyond the human will. Often the meaning of soul is related to a fragile, perishable condition as when the soul bleeds or weeps. For example, Hyperion admits that the soul is in danger of destruction when placed in unsuitable surroundings:

> Ich wollte nun aus Deutschland wieder fort. Ich suchte unter diesem Volke nichts mehr, ich war genug gekränkt, von unerbitt-lichen Beleidigungen, wollte nicht, dass meine Seele vollends unter solchen Menschen sich verblute. (p. 163)

> I now wanted to leave Germany. I sought nothing more amongst these people. I was sickened enough from inexorable insults and didn't want my soul to bleed to death amongst such men.

Hyperion is referring to modern Germany, which lacking the glory of an ancient classical Greece, alienates the soul.

Just as in Wordsworth, we have in his German contemporary the images of prison, covering, and frost suggesting barriers to the movement of the soul. In the lyrical drama of *Empedokles*, for example, the hero pictures the soul consumed by frost and affected by inclement weather:

> Es würde Nacht und kalt
> Auf Erden und in Not verzehrte sich
> Die Seele, sendeten zu Zeiten nicht
> Die guten Götter solche Jünglinge,
> Der Menschen welkend Leben zu erfrischen. (I, v. 703–7)[6]

> It became night and cold on earth and in want the soul was consumed; the good gods ought not send such a youth to the end of time for man's withering life to be revived.

Appealing to the people of Agrigento to spare the life of a youth, he evokes the soul in the devastating scene of the Crucifixion. Earlier in the play there is reference to a world devoid of soul and spirituality as a 'seellos Schattenbild' (I, i. 45). What is soulless is pictured as dark, covered and shadowy. In fact, the notion of *die Nacht der Seele* evolves in the course of *Hyperion* and is conveyed in particular by the hero when he speaks of the deadening effects of his 'Jahrhundert':

> Es gibt ein Verstummen, ein Vergessen alles Daseins, wo uns ist, als hätten wir alles verloren, eine Nacht unsrer Seele, wo kein Schimmer eines Sterns, wo nichts einmal ein faules Holz uns leuchtet. (p. 44)

> There is a dumbness, a forgetting of all existence where it is to us as if we had lost all, a night of our soul, where there is no shimmer of a star, where no spark of light from under a bundle of logs ever appears.

Neither a shimmer of a star nor a spark of light from a bundle of logs of wood appears in this night, which is the ultimate barrier to the soul's activity.

Yet more often the soul is associated with a dynamic existence always in movement, impervious to human ills, invulnerable in contrast with the aching and perishable body. Its vague but very real presence is what gives the poet his assurance of the power of transcendence, of eventual passage into the orbit of 'heavenly freedom'. Just like Wordsworth, Hölderlin closely relates the vitality of the soul to the condition of childhood. In a poem entitled 'Da ich ein Knabe war' the poet binds the child's soul to nature:

> So hast du mein Herz erfreut
> Vater Helios! Und wie Endymion,
> War ich dein Liebling,
> Heilige Luna!
>
> O all ihr treuen
> Freundlichen Götter!
> Dass ihr wüsstet,
> Wie euch meine Seele geliebt![7]

> So have you gladdened my heart, Father Helios! And like Endymion was I your darling, Holy Moon! O all you faithful friendly gods! Would that you knew how my soul loved you!

In the passage through life, the soul is the force that promises eventual liberation from the body's prison and turmoil. In the poem 'Menons Klagen Um Diotima', Hölderlin alludes to the captive fate of the soul on earth:

> Immer kannst du noch nicht, o meine Seele!
>   noch kannst du's
> Nicht gewohnen, und träumst mitten in
>   eisernen Schlaf![8]

Not yet can you, o my soul, not yet can you become acclimated, and
you dream in the midst of an iron sleep.

And in 'Brot und Wein' Hölderlin refers to an imprisoned soul or
'gefangen Seele'.[9] In fact, there is a strong element of alienation, not
abated by the philosophic mind of a Wordsworth. In one instance the
estrangement is vividly expressed through the image of a fish out of its
element: in *Hyperion*, the hero separated from his beloved, Diotima,
writes to his friend Bellarmin:

> Meine Seele ist, wie ein Fisch aus ihrem Elemente auf den Ufersand
> geworfen, und windet sich und wirft sich umher, bis sie vertrocknet
> in der Hitze des Tags. (p. 61)

> My soul is like a fish cast away from its element onto a sand dune,
> and it writhes and flings itself about until it dries up in the heat of
> the day.

In the simile of the soul as a fish dried up in the heat, Hyperion conveys
his own bitter depression in terms of the frustration of the soul on earth.
In contrast to the heavenly sphere of Diotima, an infernal character is
attributed to the soul which writhes in agony in its dwelling on earth.
The physical sensation of heat is metaphoric of the suffocation of the
soul in the domain of the earth.

Sometimes the soul bursting from its temporary abode appears to
exceed its capacity to coexist with the physical body: in one instance,
Hölderlin uses the expression 'zu reif geworden' ['became too ripe'] in
speaking of the soul, implying a time allotment for maturation and
passage and a desire to speed up the process. This expression is put in
the mouth of Diotima as she struggles with a soul which is no longer
suited for existence on earth:

> Oder ist mir meine Seele zu reif geworden in all den Begeisterungen
> unserer Liebe und hält sie darum mir nun, wie ein übermütiger
> Jüngling, in der bescheidenen Heimat nicht mehr? (p. 152)

> Or did my soul become too ripe for me in all the rapture of our love
> and therefore, like a wanton youth, no longer could be kept in the
> humble native dwelling?

In general, the soul runs full cycle. A clear organic analogy is finally
developed in the course of Hölderlin's poetics, best expressed in the
closing lines of 'Menons Klagen um Diotima' as 'ein Jahr der Seele'.
The soul cyclically undergoes a process of decay and fruition. When,
therefore, Empedokles, in forseeing renewal in a future golden age,
speaks of the collective soul, it is in terms of a plant springing up in
fruit and flower:

> Und dringt in Zweig und Frucht die neue Seele. (II, iv. 1624)

It becomes clear that around the notion of soul Hölderlin delimits his combat with earthly existence and his nostalgia for the afterlife. This is a typical Romantic stance, carried to extreme dimensions:

> Die Seele war vorausgeeilt, und hatte die irdischen Glieder verlassen. Ich hörte nicht mehr und vor dem Auge dämmerten und schwankten alle Gestalten. Der Geist war schon bei Diotima. (p. 74)

> The soul had hurried ahead and had foresaken the earthly limbs. I heard no more, and before my eyes all forms dimmed and swayed. The spirit was already with Diotima.

But Hölderlin's soul as seen in *Hyperion* is not a lonely soul like that of Chateaubriand's René. It reaches out not only toward other spheres but toward *the other*, in this case, the beloved Diotima. In the framework of love, the soul is envisaged as an object which is surrendered entirely to the loved one; Hyperion exclaims that he gave his soul into the hand of his beloved: 'O du! rief ich und stürzt ihr mach, und gab meine Seele in ihre Hand in unendlichen Küssen' (p. 77). The soul, then, is envisaged as the capacity of one psyche to relate to another, to seek and to find its *alter ego*; it is the soul and not the heart that has the power of communication and the power of love:

> Wir waren Eine Blume nur, und unsre Seelen lebten in einander, wie die Blume, wenn sie liebt, und ihre zarten Freuden im verschlossnen Kelche verbirgt. (p. 64)

> We were but one flower, and our souls lived in each other as the flower, when in love, hides its tender joys in its closed cup.

The typically Romantic notion of soul-mate is highlighted in Hyperion's meeting with Diotima, who is pictured more divine than human.

The soul is also, in Hölderlin, the seat of the sense of aesthetic values; it is the soul (not the eyes, nor the mind) that conceives ideal Beauty. Hyperion states:

> Ich hab es Einmal gesehn, das Einzige, das meine Seele suchte, und die Vollendung, die wir über die Sterne hinauf entfernen, die wir hinausschieben bis ans Ende der Zeit, die hab ich gegenwärtig gefühlt. Es war da, das Höchste ... o ihr, die ihr das Höchste und Beste sucht, in der Tiefe des Wissens, im Getummel das Handelns, im Dunkel der Vergangenheit, im Labyrinthe der Zukunft, in den Gräben oder über den Sternen! wisst ihr seinen Namen? den Namen des, das Eins ist und Alles? Sein Name is Schönheit. (pp. 54–5)

> I have seen it once, the only one that my soul sought, and the perfection, that we place beyond the stars, that we push out to the end of Time, that which I have presently felt. There it was, the highest one ... O you, who seeks the Highest and the Best, in the

deep of knowledge, in the tumult of action, in the darkness of the past, in the labyrinth of the future, in the graves or beyond the stars! Do you know its name? The name of that which is the One and All? Its name is Beauty.

The soul thus appears to become a filter between the mind and the senses and between the notion of beauty and the notion of the divine.

However, as we have noted in Wordsworth, so in Hölderlin as well, the soul does not have any unity of philosophical concept. In both cases the notion of soul lacks specific or limited signification. If on the one hand it has a personal identity, as we have seen with both Wordsworth and Hölderlin, it also has for both of them a universal collective connotation when it is more loosely used to describe the heart, the centre, or the essence of things. In that sense it is often linked with abstract qualities such as freedom and beauty, and at times it suggests even a central force in the Universe. As we have seen, it is used in connection with the animistic communicating Universe in which God is manifest.

Wordsworth blatantly evokes the 'soul's immensity' and associates the grandiose soul with the philosopher or 'Eye among the blind' in the 'Intimations' ode. This metaphoric visual power is also manifest in 'Tintern Abbey' in a passage in which the soul is depicted as totally dissolving the body as it contacts the divine and perceives it:

> that serene and blessed mood,
> In which the affections gently lead us on, –
> Until, the breath of this corporeal frame
> And even the motion of our human blood
> Almost suspended, we are laid asleep
> In body, and became a living soul:
> While with an eye made quiet by the power
> Of harmony, and the deep power of joy,
> We see into the life of things. (41–9)

In this context it is to be noted that Wordsworth, speaking of the soul, uses the first person plural, 'we' and not 'I'. In *The Prelude* Wordsworth refers to the soul of nature from which the 'sentiment of being' is derived.

> Wisdom and Spirit of the universe!
> Thou Soul that art the eternity of thought,
> That givest to forms and images a breath
> And everlasting motion, not in vain
> By day or star-light thus from my first dawn
> Of childhood didst thou intertwine for me
> The passions that build up our human soul;
> Not with the mean and vulgar works of man,

But with high objects and enduring things –
With life and nature ... (I, 401–10)

According to Wordsworth, then, the universal soul is the totality, the emanating source of life, which incarnates the permanent design of nature.

Hölderlin evokes the soul as the 'beauty of the world':

> O Seele! Seele! Schönheit der Welt! du unzerstörbare! du entzück-
> ende! mit deiner ewigen Jugend! du bist; was ist denn der Tod und
> alles Wehe der Menschen? (p. 166)

> O soul! Soul! Beauty of the world! You indestructible one! You
> delightful one! With your eternal youth! So you are. What then is
> death and all the woes of men?

In this case, soul, referring to beauty, has closer identification with Greek than with Christian deity. In fact, Hyperion, facing an impending battle in the modern world between the new Greeks and the Turks, superimposes on the event his nostalgia for the golden age and the primal state of the soul:

> Der Mensch kann nicht verleugnen, dass er einst glücklich war, wie
> die Hirsche des Forsts und nach unzähligen Jahren klimmt noch in
> uns ein Sehnen nach den Tagen der Urwelt, wo jeder die Erde
> durchstreifte, wie ein Gott, eh, ich weiss nicht was? den Menschen
> zahm gemacht, und noch, statt Mauern und totem Holz, die Seele
> der Welt, die heilige Luft allgegenwärtig ihn umfing. (pp. 116–17)

> Man cannot deny that he was once happy like the stag of the
> forest, and after countless years there yet rises in us a longing for
> primal times when each one roamed the earth as a god, ere I know
> not what made men tame and, instead of stone walls and dead wood,
> the soul of the world, the omnipresent holy air still embraced him.

Infused with the soul of the world and breathing sacred air, man becomes a demi-god as in ancient times. Here, the soul is not a personal possession carried over from a previous existence as in the Ode of Wordsworth, but the heavenly air which man breathes. In this way, Hölderlin opposes the static, lifeless character of man's ordinary life, suggested by the wall and the dead wood, with the vital life principle of the soul in its unity and totality. Again, an impersonal tone is conveyed, this time through the use of the word 'Man', instead of 'I'.

In Hölderlin we also find the typical attitude of the Romantic notion of Nature as a temple, the poet as a functioning priest, performing communion between the individual soul and the collective one in Nature. Whereas we found the human soul mobile, not enclosed but surging toward another structure, the soul of Nature is viewed as a stable, invariable entity.

As in Wordsworth, so in Hölderlin the word 'soul' is then multifaceted: personal, interpersonal, associated with the spirit of the world, and containing the collective psyche.

The imagery relating to the soul and the general sense of soul in the works of these two major Romantic poets is typical rather than exceptional. In the poetry of other notable poets of the period such as Lamartine, Eichendorff and Brentano, we find imagery reminiscent of Wordsworth and Hölderlin. The movement of the soul from construction to freedom, clearly identifiable in the patterns of the chain and prison metaphors on the one hand, and on the other in the metaphors of its eventual deliverance is not disturbed by the intrusion of other types of imagery. The direction of the soul common to these poets is that of ascent and elevation. The imagery and metaphoric language tend to paraphrase the Christian's affirmation of the immortality of the soul after life. In fact, the importance of the soul in relation to the body is so dominant that it colours the poet's perspective towards the life of the here and now and of the transcendent hereafter. As we read the poems in sequence we realize that the soul is interchangeable with the 'I' in the lyrical expression of presence, feeling and eventual departure.

We note, for instance, that the chain and prison complex is central to a poem such as Lamartine's 'Dieu' of *Les Méditations* (1821) and figures in the poet's expression of the soul's incompatability with the earth and transcendence in the other world of the 'l'au-delà':

> Oui, mon âme se plaît à secouer ses chaînes:
> Déposant le fardeau des misères humaines,
> Laissant errer mes sens dans ce monde des corps,
> Au monde des esprits je monte sans efforts.
> Là, foulant à mes pieds cet univers visible,
> Je plane en liberté dans les champs du possible.
> Mon âme est à l'étroit dans sa vaste prison:
> Il me faut un séjour qui n'ait pas d'horizon. (p. 74)[10]

Yes, my soul delights in shaking off her chains; relieving herself of the burden of human miseries, letting my senses wander in the world of bodies, I rise effortlessly to the world of the spirit. There, casting down the visible universe, I soar in liberty in the fields of the possible. My soul is constrained in its vast prison: I need an abode without a horizon.

In fact, so obtrusive is this concept of soul in Lamartine's poetry that it invades the 'I' with its spirituality. It is therefore no longer even necessary for Lamartine to mention the word in speaking of immortality. The confusion of the soul and the 'I' is evident in the following lines from 'L'Immortalité', a poem suggestive of Wordsworth's 'Intimations' ode, where the prison and chains express the constraints of the spirit-ualized 'I':

> Viens donc, viens détacher mes chaînes corporelles,
> Viens, ouvre ma prison; viens, prête-moi tes ailes
> Que tardes-tu? Parais; que je m'élance enfin
> Vers cet être inconnu, mon principe et ma fin. (p. 17)

> Come then, come remove my corporal chains, come open my prison; come, lend me your wings. Why do you delay? Appear, so I finally soar toward this unknown being, my beginning and my end.

We notice the familiar image of the earth as place of temporary exile, in, for example, Lamartine's poem 'L'Isolement':

> Que ne puis-je, porté sur le char de l'Aurore,
> Vague objet de mes voeux, m'élancer jusqu'à toi!
> Sur la terre d'exil pourquoi resté-je encore?
> Il n'est rien de commun entre la terre et moi. (p. 4)

> Would that I could, carried on the chariot of dawn, vague object of my desires, surge forth toward you! Why do I yet remain in the land of exile? There is nothing in common between the earth and myself.

Often in early Romantic poetry the succinct image of the bird is used to convey the soul's flight to the other-world. Take, for example, Eichendorff's 'Mondnacht', in which the soul is clothed in the metaphor of a bird spreading its wings as it commences a flight over the still land: a gesture which suggests a return to the divine homeland:

> Es war, als hätt' der Himmel
> Die Erde still geküsst
> Dass sie im Blütenschimmer
> Von ihm nun träumen müsst.

> Die Luft ging durch die Felder
> Die Ahren wogten sacht,
> Es rauschten leis die Wälder,
> So sternklar war die Nacht.

> Und meine Seele spannte
> Weit ihre Flügel aus,
> Flog durch die stillen Lande,
> Als flöge sie nach Haus.[11]

> It was as if the heaven had kissed the silent earth, and earth in gleams of blossoms now of heaven must dream. The air blew through the fields, the ears slight movements made, rustling gently were the woods, and starlit was the night. And so my soul did stretch her wings wide out, and flew through silent land as if she flew to God.

The destination of the soul-bird is 'nach Haus', a German expression for God. And the soul becomes what Eichendorff elsewhere called 'Paradiesvögel' in its flight toward paradise. The 'spannte' gesture clearly defines the soul's soaring.

Finally, in Brentano we find a striking instance of that familiar pattern of the soul's departure for an eternal homeland. The code expressions in this context are 'kehren', suggestive of the notion of return, and 'die Ferne', the designation of the faraway land. As expressed in a particularly nostalgic manner in the poem 'West Säuseln; Silbern Wallen' from *Godwi* (1799), final peace is granted to the restless striving soul in the long-awaited journey ('ersehnten Reisen') towards God:

> Bald, ach bald wird bessres Leben
> Dieses müde Herz erfreun,
> Und der Seele banges Streben
> Ewig dann gestillet sein.
> Schwarzer Grabesschatten dringet
> Um den Tränenblick empor,
> Aus des Todes Asche ringet
> Schönre Hoffnung sich hervor.
>
> Meines Kindes Klage hallet
> Durch Gewölbe dumpf und hohl,
> Idolmios Zunge lallet
> Jammernd mir das Lebewohl
> Zu der lang ersehnten Reise.
> Senkt mich in der Toten Reihn.
> Klaget nicht, denn saft und leise
> Wird des Müden Schlummer sein.[12]

Soon, ah soon will a better life cheer this weary heart, and the soul's restless striving will then eternally be stilled. Dark shadows of the grave well forth in the tearful eye, and from out the ashes of death brighter Hope issues forth. My lament of the Child echoes through vaults dark and hollow, my idol's tongue mumbles a bewailing farewell for the long awaited journey. Cast me in the death row. Grieve not, for the slumber of the weary will be soft and light.

Here, then, are instances of salient words, expressions, and imagery which confirm the early Romantics' notion of soul. The passwords haunt us: 'l'au-delà', 'Ewigkeit', 'planer', 'spannen'. Glaring are the contrasts between the chain-prison complexes suggesting constraint on the one hand, and the wings, birds and ethereal chariots, suggestive of release, on the other. Finally, there is the fundamental motif of journey containing sub-motifs of the exile, migration through flight, and the

return home. The entire pattern reveals a kinship in these poets' transcendent attitude toward the soul.

Regardless of their national framework, these Romantic poets are
grounded in the common Christian dogmas of the affiliation of the soul
with Christian immortality. What is therefore notable in gleaning
through these works is not the common philosophy but its crystallization in the elaboration of the metaphoric spectrum.

Not all Romantic poets, however, follow the standard pattern. There
are some blatant exceptions and variations which in a sense will be seen
in lyrical expressions of the soul in the rest of the century. Particularly
in the case of Novalis and Jean-Paul we find a new dimension to the
standard Romantic topography of the soul – which is the descent and
the recess of the dream. The two works in which this is most evident
are Novalis' *Heinrich von Ofterdingen* and Jean-Paul's *Titan*, both
written in 1802.

There are no succinct major metaphors regarding the soul in Novalis'
poetic writings. In effect his notion of soul is so englobing and total that
it does not allow itself to be expressed in small metaphoric structures.
The word *Seele* is to be distinguished from other spiritual principles
such as *Geist* and *Gemüt* which appear more frequently in the poet's
actual language. Both these words bear a connotation which relates
them to a more theologically oriented strain of Novalis' poetic writings
such as the *Geistliche Lieder* of his later years. When Novalis uses the
word soul in the last of the *Geistliche Lieder*, 'Ich sehe dich in tausend
Bildern', a poem addressed to the Virgin Mary, it is heavily invested
with Catholicism:

> Ich sehe dich in tausend Bildern
> Maria, lieblich ausgedrückt
> Doch keins von allen kann dich schildern
> Wie meine Seele dich erblickt. (p. 177)[13]

> I see you in a thousand images, Mary, lovingly expressed, yet none
> of them can picture you as my soul envisions you.

The word *Geist* relates more closely to a spiritual principle defined by
air. *Gemüt* refers to a spirituality which defines character, and the
adjective 'gemütlich' is descriptive of the eighteenth-century Christian
humanist characters found, for example, in *Heinrich von Ofterdingen*.
It suggests good-naturedness, generosity and general well-being.

When we come to the concept of soul, we are drawn into a darker
strain of Novalis' poetic writings which involves the alchemical probing
of the universe. The quality most characteristic of the soul is *depth*.
The key to Novalis' concept of soul is to be found in the first of the six
Hymnen an die Nacht. In the opening lines the poet refers to the

'innerste Seele', and accordingly emphasizes the superlative degree of interiority by which the soul is characterized. The most characteristic kingdom of the soul is the mysterious and fertile region of the night. In turning away from the light of the day, the poet proceeds to define the region of the soul. The world covered by the night is the Orphic underworld, and emphasis is placed on its depth:

> Fernab liegt die Welt – in einen tief Gruft versenkt – wüst und einsam ist ihre Stelle. (p. 131)

> Far-off lies the world – sunk in a deep abyss – lonesome and desolate is its place.

The symbol for the night is the mantle, a covering which conceals the source of the unseen power affecting the soul:

> Was hältst du unter deinem Mantel, das mir unsichtbar kräftig an die Seele geht? (p. 131)

> What is it that you hold under your mantle, which unseen, powerfully stirs my soul?

This designation of the soul is further developed in *Heinrich von Ofterdingen*, written two years after the *Hymnen*. Particularly pertinent to the characterization of the soul are the various descriptions of penetration into the earth found in the fifth chapter of Part I of the romance. As the disciples of Saïs had been taught to unveil the goddess Isis in their quest for the ideal, so the youth Heinrich, the allegorical poet, is instructed into the secret art of mining, the symbol of the poetic probing of the universe.

Aside from the two abstract words suggestive of the soul, 'beträchtliche Tiefe' (considerable depth) and 'geheimen Dasein' (secret being or quintessence), an entire set of images emerge as concrete correlatives of the innermost being. The fertile underworld explored by Heinrich and his aged mentor consists of hidden treasure-vaults ('verborgene Schatzkammern'), dark wonderful chambers ('dunkle, wunderbare Kammern'), collapsing abysses ('einbrechende Abgrund') and dark wide halls ('dunkle weite Hallen'). Here is the topography of the soul which seems to be identified with the subconscious. The language is characterized by words which relate to that which is hidden, secret and removed such as 'fremd', 'Geheimnis', 'entfernen', 'verdecken', 'verborgen', and 'bedecken'. At the heart of the underworld are secret precious stones ('die köstlichen Sterne') which like the secret 'Dasein' lie hidden beneath the surface and invite exploration (pp. 242–53). The entire journey is towards transparency ('Durchsichtigkeit'), a major motif in Novalis' poetic writings. Nature, and in particular the earth, is the covering or body made transparent. In its depth lies the hidden soul. This symbolism demonstrates to what extent Novalis departs from the standard pattern of the soul that we have noticed towards what we shall note as a more evolved metaphor of the soul.

The association of soul with depth and with the journey downward is fundamental to Jean-Paul's poetic vision as well. In his romance *Titan* the dream is a catalyst which dissolves the body and opens the soul. Expressions such as 'Nacht der Seele' and 'Seelen-Wiege des Schlafes' establish the kinship of soul and dream. The essential soul-metaphor which crystallizes Jean-Paul's soul concept is to be found in the 25th Jubilee entitled *Der Traum – die Reise*. It is one of the many dream episodes of the hero Albano. But where in other instances Jean-Paul focuses on the content of the dream, here he draws our attention to the transitory state of the awakening of the soul to Reality through the intermediary of dream. In contrast to the Orpheus myth which was central to Novalis, here the Endymion myth and its dream suggestiveness is appropriately invoked and associated with the hero Titan. The descent of the soul into the dream territory is revealed in the following allegorical lines:

> Den blühenden Endymion überdeckte schon Lächeln and Freuden – Glanz als ein voraufenden Morgenstein seines wachen Tags. Seine Seele ging lächelnd in den funkelnden Höhle der unterirdischen Schätze umher, die der Geist des Traums aufsperrt; indes das gemeine Auge des Wachens blind vor dem nahen, von Schlaf ummauerten Geister – Eldorado stand. Endlich öffnete ein unbekanntes Wonne – Ubermass Albanos Auge – der Jungling erstand sogleich mit Kraft. (pp. 551–2)[14]

> Resplendent was the fair Endymion in his smiling and his delight, bright as an advancing morning star of the waking day. His soul went laughingly about the sparkling grotto of subterranean treasures which the spirit of the dream unlocks; meanwhile the vulgar eye of waking reality was blinded in this setting, covered by a wall of sleep from the spirit's Eldorado. Finally an unknown rapture was roused in him, a visionary gleam filled his eye, and the youth emerged suddenly fraught with power.

As in the case of Novalis, the images 'funkelnden Höhle' and 'unter-dischen Schätze' are suggestive of the fertile profundity of the soul. The playfulness of Jean-Paul's poetic style is an additional element in the allegory and tends to personalize the soul: 'Seine Seele ging lächelnd.' The hero is laid to sleep in body and becomes a living soul.

The dream scenario which the hero describes is the typical Jean-Paulian setting, best described at the beginning of *Titan*. We have the familiar pattern of the boat transporting the soul to the Edenic Paradise, the contact with the soul-mate or the divine Liane and the preponderance of earthly landscape which had characterized the earlier passage of the hero on the pleasure boat to the Isola Bella in search for lost paternity, childhood and self-identity.

One of the most illuminating designations of the soul in Jean-Paul's writings is that of the 'aufgeweichte Seele' (p. 109) of the 3rd Jubilee. Translated as the mollified soul, the expression is an example of the notion of the sensuality (*Sinnlichkeit*) of the soul. Unlike Lamartine and the others aforementioned where the 'I' takes on the spirituality of the soul, here we have one of the first instances of what will evolve as a new trend: the sensualization of the soul. The expression above highlights the susceptibility of the soul to the physical. In the dream, the soul senses the spiritual through the intermediary of the physical: in particular sensations of sight, that is colours, images of nature ('feurigen Gemälden näher vor die Seele') (p. 14) and sensations of hearing ('der Gesang der Dichter und der Nachtigallen tiefer in die aufgeweichte Seele quillt') (p. 109) have an impact on the soul in a distinctly physical manner. The notion of soul finally emerging from Jean-Paul's writings is of a profound essence and sensual spirituality.

The previously discussed trend of ascendance and spirituality of the soul is then subjected in Jean-Paul and Novalis to a reversal. The soul vicariously assumes human, physical patterns as it acquires sensuality and eventually descends into the earth.

In the early Romantic context, we have viewed the soul-concept emerge at two distinct poles of the Romantic sensibility. On the one hand we have seen the powerful ascending soul, surmounting human frailties and shaking the shackles, associated in our minds with the power of the eagle and the summit of mountains. On the other hand we have detected the descending movement of soul probing the depths of being. We witness yet another attitude toward soul in the writings of two other notable early Romantics. Reference is here made to them because they forecast the direction which the soul image takes as it departs from the standard Romantic concept of it. The character of soul in von Kleist and Coleridge which illustrates this aberration is that of the soul in jeopardy.

A work thoroughly permeated with soul imagery, language relating to soul, and general sense of soul is Kleist's lyrical drama *Penthesilea* (1807). The word appears most frequently to designate the various pitches of emotion which the major figure, the Amazon queen, Penthesilea, reaches in her futile struggle to conquer the heart of Achilles.

Most often the soul is associated with the rage and violence equalled only by a powerful thunderfall. In declaring her intentions of conquest to the confident Prothoe, Penthesilea speaks of her untamed soul as a thunderbolt which cannot be controlled:

Lass mich
Du hörst, was ich beschloss, eh würdest du
Den Storm, wenn er herab von Bergen schiesst,
Als meiner Seele Donnersturz regieren. (v. 634–7)[15]

Leave me! You hear what I have decided. Sooner would you tame a torrent falling from the mountains than stay the thund'rous crash of my soul.

The rage becomes identified with the 'Hochgefühl' which confuses ('verwirrt') the soul into a state of unconsciousness:

Ich will zu meiner Füsse Staub ihn sehen
Den Ubermutige, der mir an diesem
Glorwürdgen Schlachtentag, wie keiner noch,
Das kriegerische Hochgefühl verwirrt. (v. 638–41)

I will see him humbled at my feet, that upstart, who like no other, stirs me on this glorious day of battle into a state of warlike rage.

Prothoe proceeds to describe Penthesilea's soul with the adjective 'reizen', meaning inflamed.

Another devastating image is that of a soul surrendered to pillage. In the ninth scene of the play, Kleist has the high priests say that Penthesilea's soul has been handed over to the avenging gods in language evocative of the sense of Greek tragic destiny:

Zum Raub ist ihre Seele hingegeben (ix. 1233)

To ravage is her soul surrendered.

The intensity of the feeling robs the being of consciousness.

The adjective 'matt' or weary, exhausted, is used to qualify the soul. Penthesilea, overcome by her passion, her heart torn asunder by love, exclaims:

Ach meine Seele is matt bis in den Tod. (ix. 1237)

Alas, my soul is weary unto death.

The soul stands for her entire being, which is weary, wrought by passion. It is interesting to note that the word 'matt' is also used in conjunction with the heart in the fourteenth scene where Penthesilea speaks of 'dies mattgequälte Herz'.

The various qualifications of the soul and heart point to its wounded nature. It is the innermost sensibility wounded by the arrow of love and destroyed by overwhelming passions of hate, maliciousness, and ultimately remorse which gnaws at its core.

Ruin is the soul's ultimate destiny. In fact, one of the priestesses in the closing scene speaks of the total ruin of Penthesilea's soul in a disaster which elicits the compassion of those around her:

> O eine Träne, du Hochheilge
> Die in der Menschen Brüste schleicht
> Und alle Feuerglocken der Empfindung zieht,
> Und: Jammer! rufet, dass das ganze
> Geschlecht, das leicht bewegliche, hervor
> Stürzt aus den Augen und, in Seen gesammelt,
> Um die Ruine ihrer Seele weint. (xxiv. 2783–9)

O, but what a tear, Almighty One, that steals into the breast of man, that sways all the passionate bells of feeling, and cries in woe, so that the entire race, feeble as it is, rushes forth from out our eyes, and gathered in a sea of suffering weeps for the ruin of her soul.

Like the collapsed building, a central metaphor in Kleist, the soul is the edifice that ultimately crumbles into destruction.

In Kleist's *Penthesilea*, then, the soul is coloured with the vulnerability and mortality that Kleist himself ascribed to the human condition. The closing lines of the drama, 'wie gebrechlich ist der Mensch, ihr Götter', emphasize Kleist's concept of the fragility of humankind. The quotations containing the soul gleaned from the drama depict a soul pillaged, exhausted to death, fearful, thunderous, malicious and finally ruined as the last scene contends. The soul is closely allied to the heart in its susceptibility to 'vernichtendes Gefühl', of which the most significant element is self-inflicted remorse. The final image in *Penthesilea* of an oak collapsing is Kleist's final illustration of the fate of mankind and a correlative of the ruined soul.

In Coleridge's writings, too, there is evidence of a soul endangered. To discover a poem totally focused on the soul we can go to the poet's curt but expressive *Psyche* (1808). There he refers to the traditional Greek image of the soul as butterfly. He rejects the butterfly and replaces it with its more primitive and more servile form, the reptile, stunting its metamorphic process by debasing it to the crawling stage in its earthly phase. Although other such direct allusions to soul are rare, there are clues in the language which link soul with some aspect of susceptibility to destruction.

The *Limbo* poem of 1817 will later describe the annihilation of soul by negation, nothingness or what was in the century to be called 'ennui'; it foreshadows the death-of-the-soul pattern which we will encounter and study at the end of the century. Language suggesting violence, seizure, pulverization, poisoning, shock, terror and shrinkage qualifies the soul. Here are the ominous words:

> The sole true Something – This! In Limbo's Den
> It frightens Ghosts, as here Ghosts frighten men.

Thence cross'd unseiz'd – and shall some fated hour
Be pulveris'd by Demogorgon's power,
And given as poison to annihilate souls –
Even now it shrinks them – they shrink in as Moles. (pp. 429–30)[16]

Though soul designates men in this context, nevertheless it is prone to annihilation and enclosure. Fettered as it is from flight, there is no hint of transcendence. The total feeling of stifling and suffocation is expressed most appropriately by the major image of the den:

No such sweet sights doth Limbo's den immur,
Wall'd round, and made a spirit-jail secure,
By the mere horror of blank Naught-at-all. (pp. 430–1)

We have, in this instance, an evolution of the infectious frustration of Coleridge's 'Dejection' ode. It is interesting to note that in the dialogue that is created by the simultaneous writing of Wordsworth's 'Intimations' ode and Coleridge's 'Dejection' ode, the most striking feature is indeed the diametrically opposite position taken in reference to the soul, Wordsworth's being a staff of his exhilaration and Coleridge's the shroud of his despair.

The major soul-concept in Coleridge's poetry is that of 'the soul in agony', found in the *Rime of the Ancient Mariner*. In the fourth section of the poem the anguished soul is evoked and the teeming quality of the mariner's remorse is objectified in the images relating to decay such as the rotting sea and the rotting deck:

Alone, alone, all, all alone,
Alone on a wide wide sea!
And never a saint took pity on
My soul in agony. (p. 196)

Like the mariner who kills the spirit of life, the albatross, in the Coleridgean canon the soul alienates itself from the life principle and becomes an entity of constraint and a burden. Onward it journeys like a lost pilgrim, damaged, tormented, endlessly haunted by the pains of a remorseful conscience, pursued by obsessive reminiscences of intolerable deeds. Tediously it crawls, dragging itself heavily upon the rocks and sediments of earth.

Having seen the exotic amaranth, having soared in Joy's dominion, having delved into the fertile gorges and crystalline caverns, the soul returns to the plateau of humdrum existence and restlessly wallows in its emptiness. There it encounters the parsimonious monotony of space and the dull syndrome of time. Longingly it seeks winds of inspiration or the purging of unconsciousness to relieve it of the torment that it inflicts upon itself. Desperately it wishes to flee, not from an exterior agent but from its own being.

The motions described above suggest that the soul in Coleridge has already lost the virginal quality that was so intrinsic to the Wordsworthian soul. The wayward, disturbed soul of Coleridge has contact with a phase of existence of which Wordsworth was oblivious. Nor were the dreamoriented Germans, Novalis and Jean-Paul, enslaved by the human predicament with which Coleridge became closely involved. In the coming pages it is to be seen how the direction of the soul will move towards humanization, as in the case of the faltering Coleridge, and gradually will surrender the pattern of transcendence set by the early Romantics.

3 Shelley and Keats: the Battling Soul

When we come to consider the use of the notion of soul in Shelley and Keats a distinct variation becomes evident in the very language that denotes 'soul'. Although the duality between the physical and the spiritual existence is still present, the perfectibility of the physical rather than its rejection characterizes the afterlife of the soul. The frame of reference is not the Christian dichotomy but the notion of a Pagan Elysium in which the spiritual is embodied in the physical to create an ideal state. In adhering to this pagan view, both Shelley and Keats heighten the elements relating to man and his natural, earthly land-scapes in order to suggest the eventual ideal. Both poets ignite the soul with the spark of human beauty and feeling. They replace the abstract characteristics usually associated with the soul by concrete attributes connected generally with the physical being. In this way, the soul-metaphors to be examined in the sampling from the poetry of Shelley and Keats assume a human[1] aspect, knitting together all the spiritual longings and aspirations into a network of a keen sensual apparatus.

The main difference, as we shall observe, between the two poets' handling of the soul, is that in Shelley the notion of soul in body is generally a pleasurable one, whereas in Keats it assumes more of a character of pain, confinement, frustration at the core of being.

In the general critical literature[2] relating to Shelley and Keats the emphasis has been on their conceptual ideas and their relationship to Platonism. The notion of soul in Keats' 'Ode to Psyche' and Shelley's *Epipsychidion* could be discussed in terms of philosophy. But simply to repeat what others have painstakingly detected would be a deviation from the focus of this study. Rather than speculating upon the rational processes or human vicissitudes that lead to the two poets' expression of soul, we will pursue the crystallization of attitudes toward the soul. The two works that are most revealing from this perspective are: *Endymion* (1818) and *Prometheus Unbound* (1820). These works, therefore, will be the object of our major preoccupation.

Let us start by considering the common grounds upon which the notion of soul is established in the poetry of these two poets. In both the sense of soul reaches its highest awareness in human love where the masculine and the feminine communicate through the unifying element of the soul. In both Keats' *Endymion* and Shelley's *Prometheus Un-*

bound ideal love is often translated into human terms and the soul becomes the link between the lovers. In *Endymion*, the youth's love of the divine moon goddess is transferred to the human object of love represented by the Indian maid; the love-image preserves its quasi-divine quality by using the meeting of souls as the intermediary between divine love and human love. John Middleton Murry has appropriately observed in reference to the Indian Maid the tightening of the connection between body and soul in love.[3] Similarly, in *Prometheus Unbound*, the soul becomes the essential point of union between the lovers, Prometheus and Asia. A statement made by the Moon in *Prometheus Unbound* corroborates the notion of the soul as an instrument of fusion:

> As in the soft and sweet eclipse,
> When soul meets soul on lovers' lips . . . (IV, 450–1)[4]

A strikingly similar designation of the soul is evident in the following passage from *Endymion*:

> but who, of men, can tell
> That flowers would bloom, or that green fruit would swell
> To melting pulp, that fish would have bright mail,
> The earth its dower of river, wood, and vale . . .
> If human souls did never kiss and greet? (I, 835–8; 842)[5]

Here Keats advisedly refers to the soul as human, bringing to the word all the physical pains and pleasures associated with the human condition. The soul is associated with the physical kiss. It is also to be noted that the soul is evoked in a natural setting. Keats situates the soul in a physical environment and involves it in physical love. Keats states:

> Melting into its radiance, we blend,
> Mingle, and so become part of it,
> Nor with aught else can our souls interknit
> So wingedly. (I, 810–13)

In this instance the words 'melting', 'mingle', and 'interknit' are linked to the soul, thereby rendering physical properties to the soul. An even stronger evocation of the power of love is found in a passage at the beginning of Book III of *Endymion:*

> Yet, in our very souls, we feel amain
> The close of Troilus and Cressid sweet. (II, 12–13)

The soul is here placed in the framework of an earthly love experience, suggested by the mention of Troilus and Cressid, a couple identified in literary allusions as a symbol of sensual love.

Shelley's *Epipsychidion* offers yet another powerful example of the soul set in a network of concrete, earthly references. Once again the soul is a meeting ground for physical and spiritual love. The poet, singing an 'invitation to voyage' to his loved one whom he wishes to transport to an island in Elysium, foresees his union with his beloved in these terms:

> Our breath shall intermix, our bosoms bound
> And our veins beat together; and our lips
> With other eloquence than words, eclipse
> The soul that burns between them, and the wells
> Which boil under our being's inmost cells,
> The fountains of our deepest life, shall be
> Confused in Passion's golden purity,
> As mountain-springs under the morning sun.
> We shall become the same, we shall be one
> Spirit within two frames, oh! wherefore two? (565–74)

The allusion is clearly to ideal love. The expression is in earthly terms. A series of concrete words surrounds the word 'soul' There are those suggestive of the close contact of physical love such as 'breath', 'bosoms', 'veins', and 'lips'. There are those words relating to physical phenomena which make the experience of paradise an earthly one: 'wells', 'fountains', 'mountain-springs', and 'morning sun'. Finally, the physical sensation of burning is attributed to the soul. It is clear that these details colour the abstract notion of soul in vividly concrete imagery. Furthermore, the word 'soul', presented in its singular form, contrasts with the plural form of 'bosoms', 'veins', 'lips', 'them', and 'cells', in this way representing a unifying force. It is to this unity that Shelley alludes in a subsequent passage:

> One hope within two wills, one will beneath
> Two overshadowing minds, one life, one death
> One Heaven, one Hell, one immortality,
> And one annihilation. (584–7)

In Keats' poetry the soul is the innermost being conveying the physical and the spiritual in their composite totality, as can be illustrated in the following passage where Endymion speaks:

> Now I have tasted her sweet soul to the core,
> All other depths are shallow: essences,
> Once spiritual, are like muddy lees,
> Meant but to fertilize my earthly root. (II, 904–7)

The key words which express the nature of the soul in this passage are 'core', 'depths', and 'essences'. Through these words the soul is presented as 'I' in its integral sense. The penetration of the soul through the senses to the depth of being, in this instance through the sense of taste, attributes to the soul a distinctly physical quality. The soul is being at its greatest intensity and depth. The particular word 'depth' connects the soul with the earthly since 'depth' implies that which is deeply embedded. The movement into the soul is one of descending rather than ascending and therefore underlies the notion of the soul as essentially earthbound. The association of the soul with depth and interiority is particularly lucid in one of Keats' sonnets 'To Sleep', in which the poet speaks of the soul as contained within a casket to be closed by sleep:

> Turn the key deftly in the oiled wards,
> And seal the hushed Casket of my soul.

In 'The Ode on Melancholy', it is through the sense of taste that Keats approaches the soul. There, the soul, fully open to the anguish of waking reality, is evoked in physical terms. It is the soul that implements the union of the concrete and the abstract: 'His soul shall taste the sadness of her might.'

Both Keats and Shelley associate the soul with a concrete sense of hearing as well. But if the sense of taste drew the soul into earthly dimensions, music as it affects the physical sense of hearing invades the soul with echoes of the divine. In Book III of *Endymion*, the youth hears the lyre of his beloved and falls under the spell of the heavenly music:

> Thus she link'd
> Her charming syllables, till indistinct
> Their music came to my o'er-sweeten'd soul. (III, 443–5)

A similar illustration in Shelley of the soul's power of hearing can be noted in the following passage from the final act of *Prometheus Unbound*. It is Ione who speaks as a new world is born with love and harmony:

> Listen too
> How every pause is filled with under-notes,
> Clear, silver, icy, keen, awakening tones,
> Which pierce the sense and live within the soul,
> As the sharp stars pierce winter's crystal air
> And gaze upon themselves within the sea. (IV, 189–93)

Here sound is received by the inner recesses of the soul after it passes through the sense of hearing just as the stars pass through the atmosphere to reach their deep reflection in the sea. The soul is thus linked with the earth in this analogy. The passage of the notes of the divine music through the sense to the soul also serves to link soul with sense since one is envisaged as the gateway into the other. An interconnection between sense and soul is clearly established.

There are numerous instances in the poetry of Keats and Shelley in which the soul is described through physical analogies. In this respect it is to be noted that in Shelley the mingling of the soul with the material is more frequently expressed in similies than in Keats. In fact, the matrix of the union is the poetic analogy, a device admirably suited to convey a sense of union and correspondence.

In *Epipsychidion* Shelley describes his soul, which is estranged from his beloved: '. . . my soul was as a lamp-less sea', and then proceeds to attribute tempest and frost to the sea. Through the metaphor which suggests his own lack of direction, the poet links soul with a physical term 'sea'. At another point in the same poem, Shelley compares the soul in its conglomerate character[6] to a buried lamp in alluding to an isle in Elysium:

> Yet, like a buried lamp, a Soul no less
> Burns in the heart of this delicious isle,
> An atom of th'Eternal, whose own smile
> Unfolds itself, and may be felt, not seen
> O'er the gray rocks, blue waves, and forests green,
> Filling their bare and void interstices. (477–82)

In *Endymion*, Keats writes in reference to the 'Love's self': '. . . but who/Look full upon it feel anon the blue/Of his fair eyes run liquid through their souls?' (II, 542–4). Here the earthly dimension of the soul is stressed as the soul is associated with the physical element of 'liquid'.

In Keats, a pattern can be discerned in which the soul is generally depicted as feeling pain and deep confinement. In the 'Ode on Melancholy', for example, the emphasis is on a soul that suffers; Keats speaks of 'the wakeful anguish of the soul'. In 'The Eve of Saint Agnes' the soul's suffering is described in highly physical terms. In reference to the maiden Madeline Keats writes: '. . . the poppied warmth of sleep oppress'd/Her soothed limbs, and soul fatigued away.' The soul is conveyed as being subject to an earthly sensation of fatigue, a sensation generally associated with the body. When Keats has Porphyro say 'so my soul doth ache', the situation of the soul in a state of suffering is explicitly registered as physical suffering in which the spiritual totally partakes. In *Lamia*, there are expressions of the entanglement and trammelling of the soul. When Lycius tells Lamia how he is striving to bind her soul in love, we find the image of the labyrinth connected with the soul:

> How to entangle, trammel up and snare
> Your soul in mine, and labyrinth you there
> Like the hid scent in an unbudded rose (II, 51–3)

In *Endymion* the soul's suffering is presented metaphorically as a movement inward, as can be seen in the following passage:

He could bear no more, and so
Bent his soul fiercely like a spiritual bow,
And twang'd it inwardly ... (IV, 846–8)

Its agony is communicated through the image of the bow fiercely bent. Although Keats qualifies the bow as 'spiritual', the physical bending of the bow graphically translates a state of intense pain resembling a physical contortion and gives primacy to the concrete character of the image.

The confinement of the soul in the body is sustained through other instances. For example, at the moment when the Indian maid disappears in the fourth book of *Endymion*, Keats writes of the soul:

There lies a den,
Beyond the seeming confines of the space
Made for the soul to wander in and trace
Its own existence, of remotest glooms. (512–15)

The linking of the words 'confines' and 'space' creates in our mind a juxtaposition of contraries, since space by itself spontaneously suggests lack of limitation; Keats, however, reduces the meaning of the word to suggest confinement as he rations the area in which the soul may move. Another passage following the one just cited points further to the soul trapped in the world. Endymion cries:

O destiny!
Into a labyrinth now my soul would fly,
But with thy beauty will I deaden it. (629–31)

In this passage there is a split metaphor associating incongruously the word 'fly' with 'labyrinth'; this ironically proves the inability of the soul to soar.

We tend to conclude from the examinations of soul metaphors that Keats in his consideration of the soul identifies it with that precious essence in his corporeal being which is imprisoned, subjected to physical experiences and unable to separate itself from them. When we view these images, however, in the framework of his total poetry, it becomes apparent that Keats does not succumb totally to a materialistic destiny. There is internal struggle against the notion of mortal finality, and the soul's resilience is on the side of hope. Particularly dramatic is the expression of this conflict in 'Sleep and Poetry' where the chariot image of movement represents the vestiges of the transcendent. Although the chariot is conjured in the dream framework, nevertheless Keats keeps the image alive upon reawakening:

The visions all are fled – the car is fled
Into the light of heaven, and in their stead

A sense of real things comes doubly strong,
And like a muddy stream, would bear along
My soul to nothingness: but I will strive
Against all doubtings, and will keep alive
The thought of that same chariot, and the strange
Journey it went. (155–62)

In contrast to Keats, the phenomenon of the soul in body in Shelley's poetry is exhilarating. Whereas Keats alludes to the subjugation of the soul to the confines of the body, Shelley generally focuses on the soul as a creative force which actively spurs the body toward freedom. In *Prometheus Unbound*, the notion of the soul as an active force which resists restraint is conveyed through the juxtaposition of the soul with the force represented by Jupiter. The only threat to the tyranny inherent in Jupiter is the soul of man. Jupiter refers to this force which surpasses his:

All else had been subdued to me; alone
The soul of man, like unextinguished fire,
Yet burns towards heaven with fierce reproach, and doubt,
And lamentation, and reluctant prayer,
Hurling up insurrection, which might make
Our antique empire insecure . . . (III, i. 4–9)

The soul is the seat of man's rebellion against the powers that have consigned to him the human chains. It is to be noted that in its rebellion, the soul does not rebel against something that is alien to it; that is why in Shelley we can consider the soul as an integral part of the human element. Whereas Keats depicted the soul in the image of the bow as turning inward to passively suffer, in Shelley's poetry the soul erupts in the guise of an uncontrollable volcano. Furthermore the soul, rather than ascending to a heaven of Christian connotation, as it would in the poetry of Wordsworth and Hölderlin, conspires against the heaven which in Shelley's poetry is often a pagan one inhabited by the gods. The soul, then, is distinctly connected with the earth as a fire which is kindled in the bowels of the earth.

Shelley conveys the notion of soul in body as pleasurable in another passage in *Prometheus Unbound*, in which he links the word 'soul' with the word 'harmonious', thereby suggesting the concordance rather than the discordance of soul in body:

Man, one harmonious soul of many a soul,
Whose nature is its own divine control. (IV, 400–1)

It is clear from these lines that the soul is the divinity inside rather than outside of the human.

In a critical analysis of *Prometheus Unbound* in *The Romantic Imagination*, C. M. Bowra concurs with an oft-repeated conclusion that there is a Platonic world-soul in Shelley's poetry. He writes:

> In the second place, Shelley had absorbed from Plato the idea of a world soul. So far from thinking that the sum of things can be divided into spirit and matter, he held that matter does not exist and that spirit is the only reality; that nature is no less alive than man and has, like him, a soul. For Shelley the earth and everything in it are alive and directed by an immanent principle of life.[7]

This is a general statement which fails to elaborate how the soul permeates the metaphoric structure. The emphasis is aimed at a philosophical interpretation rather than at the discovery of the means of conveying the philosophy. What is particularly striking in Shelley's presentation of the soul is the elaborate imagery with which he clothes it in his poetry.

The most striking instance of the harmonious linking of the physical and the spiritual as manifest in the soul is revealed in a passage uttered by Asia which terminates the second act of *Prometheus Unbound*. It is at the moment of Asia's awakening and her embodiment of love. Here is the first stanza of the three-stanza passage:

> My soul is an enchanted boat
> Which, like a sleeping swan, doth float
> Upon the silver waves of thy sweet singing;
> And thine doth like an angel sit
> Beside a helm conducting it,
> Whilst all the winds with melody are ringing.
> It seems to float ever, for ever,
> Upon that many-winding river,
> Between mountains, woods, abysses,
> A paradise of wildernesses!
> Till, like one in slumber bound,
> Borne to the ocean, I float down, around,
> Into a sea profound, of ever-spreading sound. (II, v. 72–84)

The soul is clothed in a triple analogy of the boat, the swan and the angel. Bowra refers to this passage but is averse to dissecting the analogy to analyse it. For him, the soul element is insignificant, and he describes it in vague terms:

> The theme is the progress of the soul in love, and it is presented in a highly imaginative way. Of course, we must not examine the details separately as if each stood for some special stage or element in the experience, but the whole idea of the enchanted journey is apt and illuminating. The impression of enchanting music and of irresistible

motion is essential to the picture. The intellectual idea has been fused with the images, and the result is that the idea has a new appeal.[8]

It seems to me, however, that the poetic analogy, in itself, communicates the union of the soul with physical reality. Through the initial metaphor of the enchanted boat, a metaphor which prevails throughout the passage, Shelley traces the movement of the soul towards paradise. The notion of paradise is significant in this context. The paradise presented here preserves the attributes of the earth. It is linked with elements of earthly landscape, such as 'mountains', 'woods', 'abysses', and 'wildernesses'. In the third stanza this particular designation of paradise is reinforced in the lines:

A paradise of vaulted bowers,
Lit by downward-gazing flowers,
And watery paths that wind between
Wildernesses calm and green. (II, v. 104–7)

The soul is in search of an earthly paradise. It would seem that the river upon which the boat floats is like the Acheron river of Greek mythology which leads to the underworld. The notion of a Pagan paradise affects the intrinsic notion of the soul. The soul is linked with the physical as both soul and body move toward Elysium.

The initial metaphor of the boat is particularly germane to Shelley's delineation of the soul. The boat image is sustained throughout the entire passage through such words as 'float', 'helm', 'many-winding river', 'sea profound', 'sail', 'course', 'pinnace', and 'boat of my desire'. The boat image suggests a break-through for the soul as it frees itself from constriction. We do not see here the static state of confinement to which the soul was subjected in Keats' poetry. The enchantment of the boat also stresses the magical, intangible quality which the soul acquires as it is liberated. It is interesting to note that the boat image is to be magnified in Rimbaud's 'Bateau Ivre', in which the free play of the poet's imagination is suggested by a boat's drunken journey along unknown regions. It is, in fact, surprising that Northrop Frye, in an essay entitled 'The Drunken Boat: The Revolutionary Element in Romanticism',[9] evokes Rimbaud's title but never makes allusion to the Romantic analogy of the boat and the soul.

In Shelley's passage, the image of the sleeping swan adds a dreamlike quality to the central boat image, and reinforces the sense of enchantment that is akin to the dream state. The experience of the soul in the metaphor of the boat is one of delight. The soul is released from confines and travels freely in this dreamlike atmosphere of subjectivity. In this passage the soul is characterized by an ethereal quality in a movement toward liberation. The 'sea profound' is suggestive of the vastness and infinitude of the region into which the soul journeys. In the course of a metaphorical journey in which exhilaration and ultimate freedom are implicit, the soul gives *élan* to human sensibility. Through the boat image, then, the soul is conveyed as a vehicle engaged in a movement toward an ideal destination which is an earthly paradise.

Indeed, the enchanted boat evolves as the most striking of the images used by Shelley to designate the soul. The image glides through his poetry incessantly and is used interchangeably with the soul. As early as *Alastor*[10] (1815) there is evidence of the centrality of boat imagery to Shelley's vision though no outright identification of soul and boat was then made. Nevertheless, the work contains the germ of the entire swan-boat complex: as the swan begins its flight, so the soul embarks on its labyrinthine journey. The most haunting movement pertaining to the soul in Shelley's poetics is, as we have seen, the spirit's bark driven along shores of the daedal earth, flowing along labyrinthine pathways, into profound oceans of exhilaration and seas of eternity.

The poet Yeats, in summing up Shelley's myth, is particularly sensitive to this major image without effectively naming it as the objectivation of the soul. He speaks of the 'wisdom of the image':

> I think too that as he knelt before an altar where a thin flame burnt in a lamp made of green agate, a single vision would have come to him again and again, a vision of a boat drifting down toward a broad river, and that voices would have told him how there is for every man some one scene, some one adventure, some one picture that is the image of his secret life, for wisdom first speaks in images, and that this one image, if he would but brood over it his life long, would lead his soul disentangled from unmeaning circumstance and the ebb and flow of the world, into that fair household where the undying gods await all whose souls have become single as flame, whose bodies have become quiet as an agate lamp.[11]

Of the English-speaking poets considered in this study the one whose language is most fully saturated with soul is Shelley. As a master of the image, Shelley was to clothe the soul in various metaphors of sea, lamp, swan, but most importantly the boat: a mortal pinnace or fragile shallop ever fragile as the lyric poet himself, but light, airy, speeding and sweeping on silver seas.

If in Keats there was less recourse to the image in the designation of soul, the metaphoric language used to describe the soul was profuse. The emphasis was decisively on the constraint of the soul; its most characteristic habitat was the den, the vale, or the labyrinth. Its most typical movement was the twisting. Caught in the labyrinth, the soul meandered in webs of constriction.

Despite the qualitative distinction discerned between Keats' and Shelley's portrait of the soul in the body, the two poets' notion of the

soul provides a distinct modification when juxtaposed with its representation in the poetry of Wordsworth and Hölderlin. Both in Keats and in
Shelley the soul is couched in topographical landscapes, advancing by
degrees to conditions comparable to Christian ecstasy, yet firmly rooted
in Pagan earthy landscapes. But where in Wordsworth the emotion, as
we have seen, is the sublime, overreaching worldly concerns, in Shelley
there is the exhilaration and ecstasy of rebellion and revolt, an energy
which is kindled in the earth and soars, battling, assaulting the heaven
above. Where in Wordsworth the soul is imperial, looming gloriously
and brooding majestically on heights and mountain peaks, in Keats the
soul is enslaved – caught, twisted, enwrapped, confined, cloistered,
writhing in chains, close to the human though aspiring to the divine.
The reason for the divergence between these two sets of Romantic poets
can be shown in the following observation: whereas in Wordsworth
and Hölderlin there is a distillation process in which the separation of
the soul from the body is imminent, in the more pagan attitudes toward
the soul, as represented in the poetry of Keats and Shelley, they are
concerned with rendering permanent the earthly perfections which the
soul manifests in the framework of the body. In seeking to isolate the
perfections they have taken us through the vagaries of the human
experience, while in Wordsworth the power of the soul is so imperial
that it has no cause for struggle in its domination over the frailties of
the body. This major division between Wordsworth, Hölderlin and
other poets following the same trend, on the one hand, and Keats and
Shelley on the other, is primarily the different philosophical and spiritual orientation of the poets. However, as we have seen, it is a distinction
which is immanent in their very language as it applies to the use of the
word 'soul'.

Furthermore, in awareness of this distinction, we can conclude that
the term 'Romantic' as applied to these poets is a vague designation
which fails to take into account a basic philosophical difference between
them. In literary history, the poets have been grouped together under
this label and their orientation has been viewed as similar. An inkling
of the distinction has been suggested in the frequent reference to the
device of synaesthesia in Keats and Shelley.[12] However, synaesthesia is
a device which reflects rather than constitutes. The distinction is deeper
than this effect of style and lies in the variation of the notion of soul. If,
as we have seen, the soul is conveyed more in earthly terms, as it is more
frequently joined to the body in the poetry of Keats and Shelley,
synaesthesia conveys this union in terms of structure. As we leave these
poets and delve into the poetry of Baudelaire and Hugo and others in
mid-century we shall see a further evolution of the notion of soul in the
direction that was taken by Keats and Shelley, as it rapidly loses its
spiritual connotation and moves toward a drastic alteration in its
meaning in European Symbolist poetry.

4 Baudelaire and his Contemporaries: the Mortal Soul

In literary history, Baudelaire is generally considered as a bridge between Romanticism and Symbolism. He has been recognized as a transitional poet by most critics. This transitional role is quite evident as far as the metaphor of the soul is concerned in Baudelaire's *Les Fleurs du Mal* (1857) particularly when it is compared with parallel images drawn from the works of his antecedents and contemporaries in the French context.

The extent to which the word 'soul' appears in Baudelaire's poetry and the variety of connotations it assumes are striking. He uses the word frequently but advisedly in very specific contexts which enable us to discern certain tendencies and implications in his allusions to the soul. Baudelaire shares with the Romantic poets studied here a spiritual nostalgia for the ideal. Baudelaire is a contemporary of Hugo, and significantly we observe that some of the best examples of the standard pattern of the soul's flight to the ideal can be found in Hugo's most powerful lyric poetry dating from the same era, *Les Contemplations* (1856). For instance, the frequency of bird images emphasize Hugo's notion of elevation. Among other examples one can cite a poem from the second book, 'Je respire où tu palpites', in which the poet writes of his beloved:

> Si tu pars, mon front se penche:
> Mon âme au ciel, son berceau,
> Fuira, car dans ta main blanche
> Tu tiens ce sauvage oiseau. (p. 115)[1]

If you depart, my brow bends down; my soul into the sky, its cradle, will flee, for in your white hand you hold this bird so wild.

This particular interpretation of the soul is a prolongation of the early Romanticism observed in Wordsworth but chronologically posterior in the French context. As we examine the notion of soul in Baudelaire, we find that in many respects he adheres to the standard Romantic connotation of soul and to the concept of elevation. A poem by that name, 'Elevation', clearly demonstrates this survival of association of soul with elevation.

As we examine the imagery in which the soul is contained, however, we notice new uses of the word. The soul's aspiration for the ideal is never more than a mortal's longing with no promise of eternity. Baudelaire's concept of reversibility in all values such as the beautiful and the ugly, the good and the evil, applies equally to the soul, giving it double direction, projecting and recoiling, ethereal and heavy, but always subject to the precarious human condition.

The groupings of the images that follow will illustrate this strong identifying character of reversibility. But whether they convey an impression of effusion or of dejection they represent the soul as perishable. In fact, the soul is led toward total destruction and becomes a dead weight, which contradicts the very meaning of the word in its original Latin root.

The fact is that in the uses of soul imagery, Baudelaire takes one step backward before surging forward to grant the soul new vistas and new contexts. In an *oeuvre* in which dichotomy is the rule rather than the exception, and in which the extremes in sensibility are the ingredient of the poetic imagination, it is not surprising that the notion of the soul ranges widely. In 'L'Invitation au Voyage' the use of the word 'soul' exemplifies one end of the spectrum. In alluding to a terrestrial paradise, Baudelaire writes:

Tout y parlerait
A l'âme en secret
Sa douce langue natale. (p. 127)[2]

There, all would speak to the soul secretly, its soft, native language.

The dichotomy of the soul and the body is suggested here by the reference to the special language of the soul. The soul escapes to an earthly paradise designated by 'there' or 'là'. Although the paradise seems to be an ideal place, distinctly separate from the world of everyday experience, the description of its landscape is nevertheless concrete and earthly.

Although we have observed Baudelaire's images of elevation of soul and sublimation of its earthly habitat, these are not persistent characteristics but exceptions. One might say that the instances just cited are archaic in relation to newer uses of the word which we shall observe, and which diverge drastically from the previous ones.

The soul undergoes a dialectical process in the poetry of Baudelaire as it vacillates between two distinct representations. On the one hand, it is a quintessence which man tries to preserve although he knows it to be ephemeral. The soul in this guise goes through a process of distillation and is purified. On the other hand, the soul is frequently embodied in an earthly substance as the wounded self. It is that part of man which is hurt by earth's ills: by solitude, by the grossness of the masses, by the weaknesses of the flesh, by a constant haunting of death, by the heavy burden of time. The outstanding characteristic of the soul in this context is, as we shall see, its utter vulnerability. It is capable of being reduced to complete devastation and is depicted in pitiful states.

The expansion of the soul is conveyed primarily through the strong sensations which lift the soul and purify it to its essence. Sensations serve to put the soul in a state of suspension. In 'La Chevelure', the soul expands through the intermingling of powerful senses which act upon it and transport it into infinity:

> Un port retentissant où mon âme peut boire
> A grands flots le parfum, le son et la couleur. (p. 101)

> A resounding port, where my soul can take deep draughts of scent, of sound, of colour.

In this poem the soul is immersed in memory through the means of the senses which are incited by the synaesthesia of perfume, sound and colour. It is endowed with the capacity to transform the initial input of sense experience into a more permanent substance which is memory. The depth of the soul is suggested through the image of the sea which pervades the entire poem and which becomes mingled with the soul. In the poem 'Parfum Exotique', a similar *sorcellerie* or magic operates on the soul and makes it receptive to exotic sensations:

> Pendant que le parfum des verts tamariniers,
> Qui circule dans l'air et m'enfle la narine,
> Se mêle dans mon âme au chant des mariniers. (p. 100)

> While the fragrance of the tamarisks, which spreads in the air and inflates the nostril, mingles in my soul with the song of the sailors.

Sense and soul are united in the common feeling of expansion. The mingling of scent and song intensifies the total experience.

In the poem 'Hymne' the soul's longing for eternity is particularly noticeable as the beloved imbues it with a sense of the eternal:

> Elle se répand dans ma vie
> Comme un air imprégné de sel.
> Et dans mon âme inassouvie
> Verse le goût de l'éternel. (p. 222)

> She permeates my life like salty air, and into my unsatiated soul spills the taste of the eternal.

The physical words 'verser' and 'goût' which are associated with the soul and its appetite for eternity create an antithesis between the physical and its aspirations for eternity which remain unfulfilled ('inassouvie').

The poem is reminiscent of Hugo's 'Extase'. However, when the two poems are juxtaposed we see that although they both demonstrate an aspiration to the eternal the difference in the language of the two poems is symptomatic of a change in attitude. Though the word *soul* is not used in Hugo's 'Extase', there is intimate union between the spiritual essence and the divine eternal:

> J'étais seul près des flots, par une nuit d'étoiles.
> Pas un nuage aux cieux, sur les mers pas de voiles.
> Mes yeux plongeaient plus loin que le monde réel.
> Et les bois, et les monts, et toute la nature,
> Semblaient interroger dans un confus murmure
>   Les flots des mers, les feux du ciel.
>
> Et les étoiles d'or, légions infinies,
> A voix haute, à voix basse, avec mille harmonies,
> Disaient, en inclinant leurs couronnes de feu;
> Et les flots bleus, que rien ne gouverne et n'arrête,
> Disaient, en recourbant l'écume de leur crête,
>   – C'est le Seigneur, le Seigneur Dieu!
>   (*Les Orientales*, XXXVII)[3]

I was alone near the waves, in a starlit night, not a cloud in the heavens, on the sea not a sail. My eyes plunged further than the real world, and the woods, and the mounts, and all of nature, seemed to question in a mixed murmur, the waves of the seas and the lights of the heavens. And the stars of gold, an infinite multitude, loud and softly, with a thousand harmonies, were saying, bowing their crowns of fire: and the blue waves, which nothing rules nor checks, were saying, rebounding the foam of their crest: 'It is the Almighty, the Almighty God.'

The soul functions through the piercing eye which is imbued with nature's manifestations of the eternal and through the attentive ear which is receptive to the harmonies of the eternal. In Baudelaire the soul's longing for eternity is couched in concrete, physical terms whereas in Hugo there is saturation with the divine presence in abstract and lofty dimensions. In the 'Hymne' we find that the eternal activates such earthy images as salt and musk. It provokes the sense of taste:

> Elle se répand dans ma vie
> Comme un air imprégné de sel

It excites the sense of smell:

> Sachet toujours frais qui parfume
> L'atmosphère d'un cher réduit,
> Encensoir oublié qui fume
> En secret à travers la nuit,

Comment, amour incorruptible,
T'exprimer avec vérité?
Grain de musc qui gis, invisible,
Au fond de mon éternité!

Ever-fresh sachet perfuming the atmosphere of a precious recess,
forgotten censer burning secretly throughout the night. Incorruptible
love, how do I express you truthfully? Grain of musk lying invisibly
in the depths of my eternity!

In Hugo's 'Extase', as in other examples from the early Romantic
context, the more lofty sensations of vision and hearing are provoked
by the eternal.

When we examine the soul's expansion in a poem such as Baudelaire's 'L'Ame du Vin', we find that there is added significance in the
distinctly physical language used to express the soul's communion with
the divine. Above all, there is the outright association of soul with the
expansion that wine provokes. The distillation process which acts on
the soul is here conveyed literally as the soul migrates from its life in
wine to that of ambrosia in what resembles an alchemic transformation.
The purification of the soul is manifest as the soul enters into the sweet
liqueur of the gods. It is characteristic of Baudelaire to evoke exotic
essences such as ambrosia, musk and benzoin, and to reveal their capacity to transport man into deeper awareness and produce expansion.
The last stanza of this poem carries the alchemic process to its fulfilment as the soul engenders the birth of poetry itself – an infinite expansion:

En toi je tomberai, végétale ambroisie,
Grain précieux jeté par l'éternel Semeur,
Pour que de notre amour naisse la poésie
Qui jaillira vers Dieu comme une rare fleur! (p. 176)

Into you will I fall, 'vegetable' ambrosia, precious seed cast by the
eternal Sower, so that of our love a poetry is born which shall spring
towards God as a rare flower!

The soul is identified as the rarefied essence:

J'allumerai les yeux de ta femme ravie;
A ton fils je rendrai sa farce et ses couleurs
Et serai pour ce frêle athlète de la vie
L'huile qui raffermit les muscles des lutteurs.

I'll light the eyes of your delighted wife, to your son I'll restore his
force and his colour, and will be, for that frail athlete of the living,
the oil which strengthens the muscles of fighters.

On the basis of the use of the word 'soul' in this poem, we can see in literal, concrete terms the etherealization of the soul.

We find that in 'L'Ame du Vin', a dislocation of the soul has occurred. The prison in which the wine is contained is the glass, and when it is liberated it migrates to man, not to the divine in the hereafter:

> Un soir, l'âme du vin chantait dans les bouteilles:
> 'Homme, vers toi je pousse, ô cher désherité,
> Sous ma prison de verre et mes cires vermeilles,
> Un chant plein de lumière et de fraternité!'

> One evening, the soul of the wine was singing in the bottles: 'Sir, towards you I send forth, o dear disinherited one, from under my prison of glass and my ruddy seals of wax, a song full of light and of fraternity!'

The divine act is granted to man in his capacity for artistic creation, and man becomes what Baudelaire had termed in his aesthetics, 'l'Homme Dieu'. What is interesting, then, is that the soul functions in the realm of the human and is the basis for the poetic act which makes of the human a divinity. Second, we observe that the soul is personified: it engages in discourse, demonstrates an effervescent personality, speaks, in particular, of a love affair. From this poem we begin to notice a significant pattern by which the soul's assumption of personality correlates with the human dimension which it acquires in the course of the century as it gradually approaches the notion of the ego and is set in the worldly context.

But where the basis of the impact of the soul on the poet in 'L'Ame du Vin' is expansion, more instances in other poems show the opposite image of the soul. More often Baudelaire expresses the calcification of the soul. This is particularly true when Baudelaire wants to suggest that the soul is deeply hurt. In the poem 'La Cloche Fêlée' the concrete image of a wounded dying man enters into the metaphoric delineation of the soul and reflects the nature of the soul depicted. In this poem, Baudelaire suggests the futility with which he views the inner dejection of the soul by associating the cracked voice of the soul with that of a wounded man who dies while expending useless efforts to rise from under a heap of dead bodies:

> Moi, mon âme est fêlée, et lorsqu'en ses ennuis
> Elle veut de ses chants peupler l'air froid des nuits,
> Il arrive souvent que sa voix affaiblie

> Semble le râle épais d'un blessé qu'on oublie
> Au bord d'un lac de sang, sous un grand tas de morts,
> Et qui meurt, sans bouger, dans d'immenses efforts. (p. 144)

As for myself, my soul is cracked, and when in its distress it would fain fill the cold night air with its song, often does its wearied voice have the likeness of the ponderous death rattle of a wounded man forgotten on the brink of a pool of blood beneath a great heap of the dead, dying there, fixed, in useless efforts.

The soul is humanized and made vulnerable. Concrete physical images translate the inner spiritual wound of the soul. The 'lac de sang' vividly emphasizes the wounded condition. The double use of the word 'fêlée' to describe both the cracked sound of the bell and the spiritual suffering of the soul succeeds in powerfully conveying the utter devastation of the soul. Finally, the entire imagery relating to death: the death rattle, the wounded man, the lake of blood and the pile of dead bodies are objective correlatives for the spiritual death of the soul and for the agony of its dejection. The total message that the poem conveys is that of a wounded soul which in struggling in vain for survival succumbs to spiritual death.

Moreover, a mood identified with the soul's suffering in Baudelaire's poetry is the spleen. It expresses a violent horror of life and overwhelming depression. In the poem 'Le Crépuscule du Soir', the soul is exposed to a hellish night which discloses the ills of human existence. In the poem the mood of horror is suggested through objects relating to sordid urban life and through references to the miseries of the sick. The poet addresses his soul in the following manner:

Receuille-toi, mon âme, en ce grave moment.
Et ferme ton oreille à ce rugissement.
C'est l'heure où les douleurs des malades s'aigrissent!
La sombre nuit les prend à la gorge; ils finissent
Leur destinée et vont vers le gouffre commun;
L'hôpital se remplit de leurs soupirs. (p. 167)

Take heed, my soul, in this grave hour, and close your ears to this bellowing. It is the hour when the suffering of sick ones is worsened. The sullen night seizes them by the throat; they cease their life's course and approach the common abyss. The hospital is filled with their sighs.

Here, as in the case of 'La Cloche Fêlée', the soul is placed in a context of sickness and death.

Another facet of the spleen which envelops the soul is expressed in the poem 'Le Portrait'. In this poem alienation and utter solitude devour the soul:

C'est affreux, ô mon âme!
Rien qu'un dessin fort pâle, aux trois crayons,
Qui comme moi, meurt dans la solitude,

Et que le Temps, injurieux vieillard,
Chaque jour frotte avec son aile rude . . . (p. 114)

It's hideous, O my soul! Nothing but a very pale drawing made with
three crayons, which like myself dies in solitude, and which Time,
abusive old man, rubs each day with his harsh wing.

Once again concrete physical imagery reflects the inner injury of the
soul. Closely identified with the poet's ego in this poem, the soul is
rendered pathetically mortal through time's ravages.

It is true that striking images of the mutilation of the soul are to be
found as well in Hugo's poetry of the same era, particularly in one of
the best known poems of *Les Contemplations*, 'Melancholia'. The
physical miseries which are presented in tableaux throughout the poem
afflict the soul. As Hugo poignantly pictures the mass of humanity
suffering from the ills of the period in a poem which prefigures the
Spleen poems of Baudelaire, we witness an arresting image regarding
the soul's dismemberment:

Les petits enfants nus tendent leurs mains funèbres;
Le crime, antre béant, s'ouvre dans ces ténèbres;
Le vent secoue et pousse, en ses froids tourbillons,
Les âmes en lambeaux dans les corps en haillons. (p. 128)

The little naked children stretch forth their funereal hands;
Crime, the gaping den, opens in this darkness; The wind shakes
and scatters, in her cold whirlings, the shredded souls in the tattered
bodies.

Like the body, the soul is subject to destruction, and the terms that
apply to it are equally physical. It is to be noted that the shattering of
the soul is expressed in the same material terms as that of the body:
'lambeaux' and 'haillons' being synonymous and connoting both
poverty and deterioration. The reference to soul in material terms will
become more and more prevalent as we proceed into the latter part of
the century. In fact, the poem can be compared to those poems in
Baudelaire's canon which point forcefully to the vulnerability of the
soul and which abound in images evoking destruction and ruin of
material entities. A fitting companion to Hugo's poem would be
Baudelaire's 'Causerie' in which the poet describes how his soul is
assaulted by his beloved. The entire poem focuses on the image of the
remnant or scrap which are the objective correlatives of the poet's soul
in the aftermath of the agony of love:

O Beauté, dur fléau des âmes, tu le veux!
Avec tes yeux de feu, brillants comme des fêtes,
Calcine ces lambeaux qu'ont épargnés les bêtes! (p. 130)

O Beauty, harsh scourge of souls, you want it! With your eyes ablaze, brilliant as in festivals, burn the remains that the beasts have spared!

In an attempt to convey the ravages of love, the poet proceeds in the four stanzas of the sonnet to chronicle four successive stages of devastation. The mistress or *femme fatale* appears in four distinct guises; the autumn sky, the ferocious beast, the pillaging immoral mob raiding a palace, and finally a plague which scourges and burns those remaining shreds of her lover's soul.

Where Hugo evokes the political miseries of the time and sets the soul in the social context, Baudelaire is concerned with the particular personal experience of his ill-fated love. But in both instances, the soul concept assumes a new dimension of vulnerability and is clothed in physical metaphor.

In a number of Baudelaire's poems the soul is tossed here and there, thrown into abysses, plunged into seas. So in Hugo, we do find a plunging soul. In 'O Gouffre', for example, we have a metaphysical rendition of the plunging soul closely linked with the cosmic eye:

O gouffre! l'âme plonge et rapporte le doute . . .
Nous contemplons l'obscur, l'inconnu, l'invisible,
Nous sondons le réel, l'idéal, le possible,
    L'être, sceptre toujours présent . . .
Nous voyons s'éclairer de lueurs formidables
    La vitre de l'éternité. (*Les Contemplations*, p. 387)

O abyss! The soul plunges and brings back doubt . . . We contemplate the obscure, the unknown, the invisible. We sound the real, the ideal, the possible. Being, ever present sceptre . . . We see the lightening of awesome gleams, the window of eternity.

But the 'gouffre' is the Pascalian abyss and remains in the domain of the abstract and the theological.

What distinguishes the plunging of the soul in Baudelaire's poetry is the fact that there is concrete territory surrounding this particular activity of the soul. Furthermore, there are elements of horror concerned with life 'here' rather than awe concerned with life 'there'. A telling symptom which points to the physicality of the sensation attributed to the soul is the vertigo rather than the celestial ecstasy of Hugo. The vertigo is the equivalent of the existential feeling of anguish which the soul endures.

'Le Flacon' and 'Le Poison' are two of Baudelaire's poems in which the soul's wound is conveyed in terms of vertigo. In 'Le Flacon' the soul is seized and controlled by memory, which throws it into a state of intense suffering. Baudelaire suggests that the memory is a painful one, of a lost love:

Voilà le souvenir enivrant qui voltige
Dans l'air troublé; les yeux se ferment; le Vertige
Saisit l'âme vaincue et la pousse à deux mains
Vers un gouffre obscurci de miasmes humains. (p. 122)

There's the intoxicating remembrance which hovers in the troubled
air; the eyes close; vertigo seizes the conquered soul and thrusts it
with both hands into an abyss darkened by human miasmas.

It is clear that the sensation of vertigo is an inner one. The eyes are
closed, and the horror goes on in the soul beneath. Such words as
'seize', 'vanquished', and 'push' emphasize the violence of the sensation. They are precise physical words which succeed in rendering concrete a metaphysical anguish. Here is a strikingly graphic portrait of a
soul that is terrorized. The two hands that act upon it give it a three-
dimensional character as a concrete object. The 'gouffre' image further
points to the abyss of nothingness into which this very real entity is
thrust. As memories are suddenly awakened in it, the soul is exposed to
a condition of dire brutality.

Furthermore, the central image of the poem, the physical flask, bears
directly upon the soul. The flask is *trapped* in a closet, *revived* when the
closet is opened, and *damned* when it is hurled into an abyss. The
attributes of the weary soul are reflected in the qualification of the aged
flask:

Quand on m'aura jeté, vieux flacon désolé,
Décrepit, poudreux, sale, abject, visquex, fêlé.

When I'm thrown out, I am an old discarded scent-bottle, that is
decrepit, dusty, dirty, abject, slimy and cracked . . .

Its mortal quality is particularly evident in reference to Lazarus who
was resuscitated not for eternity but to his original state of mortality:

Il la terrasse au bord d'un gouffre séculaire,
Où Lazare odorant déchirant son suaire
Se meut dans son réveil le cadavre spectral
D'un vieil amour ranci, charmant et sépulcral.

He throws it on the brim of a venerable abyss, where the smelly
Lazarus rending his shroud, stirs in his awaking the sceptral cadaver
of an old love that is rancid, charmed and sepulchral.

The final image of the casket in the poem ironically shows that the
resuscitation like Lazarus' is temporary and associated with death
rather than with eternal life.

In 'Le Poison' the soul receives an equally brutal treatment but from
the standpoint of forgetfulness. Baudelaire sadistically envisages his
beloved in terms of poison. The poison is personified by a beautiful

woman who seduces the poet. In the second stanza of the poem, Baudelaire refers to the power that opium has to fill the poet with a passion
which inundates the soul:

> L'opium agrandit ce qui n'a pas de bornes . . .
>   Et de plaisirs noirs et mornes
> Remplit l'âme au delà de sa capacité. (p. 122)

> Opium enlarges the limitless . . . and with dark and gloomy pleasures
> fills the soul beyond its capacity.

But the passion which the beloved evokes in the poet is a far greater
force. The poet's soul is hurt by the very pleasure which it enjoys. The
poem traces the destruction of a soul tortured by the excess of its fiery
desire. The passion which the woman elicits in the poet produces the
following phenomenon:

> Tout cela ne vaut pas le terrible prodige
>   De ta salive qui mord,
> Qui plonge dans l'oubli mon âme sans remord,
>   Et charriant le vertige,
> La roule défaillante aux rives de la mort! (p. 123)

> All of that cannot equal the aweful power of your saliva which
> gnaws; which plunges my soul remorselessly into oblivion, and
> prompting vertigo, drives it in a swoon to the shores of death!

Here again the soul is abused by an exterior force. The words 'plunge'
and 'roll' are indicative of the violent power which seizes the soul and
leads it toward ultimate devastation. The word 'vertigo' again designates the sensation of the soul. The soul is rolled toward spiritual death
and utter annihilation through its own indulgence in an overwhelming
passion.

In both 'Le Flacon' and 'Le Poison' the soul is overwhelmed and
devastated. In 'Le Poison' voluptuous pleasure seizes and rules the soul
while in 'Le Flacon' a spiritual force controls the soul. In both cases,
however, the setting of water, the abyss, and the thrust by an exterior
force are concrete manifestations of the process of annihilation which
the soul undergoes.

This destructive process in regard to the soul will be dramatically
expressed by Rimbaud in 1871 in his famous 'Lettre du Voyant' which
contains his notion of the function of the poet. There the mutilation
envisaged is of such brutal proportions as to make the soul into a
monster:

> Mais il s'agit de faire l'âme monstreuse: à l'instar des comprachicos,
> quoi! Imaginez un homme s'implantant et se cultivant des verrues
> sur le visage.[4]

But the point is to make the soul monstrous: after the manner of the Comprachicos, why of course! Imagine a man implanting and cultivating warts on his face.

The notion of a lost soul is conveyed forcefully in the poetry of Baudelaire. Once again we find that the boat is an image for the condition of the soul. But the difference between the boat image in Shelley's poetry and in Baudelaire is indicative of a change in the notion of the soul. In 'Les Sept Vieillards', Baudelaire identifies the soul with a 'vieille gabarre' or old barge which rides aimlessly on the monstrous seas:

> Vainement ma raison voulait prendre la barre;
> La tempête en jouant déroutait ses efforts,
> Et mon âme dansait, dansait, vieille gabarre
> Sans mâts, sur une mer monstrueuse et sans bords! (p. 160)

> In vain my reason would take the helm; the tempest, sporting, countered its essays, and my soul danced and danced, an old mastless barge on a monstrous sea without shores!

In this poem, the soul is thrown into a state of confusion after the poet has contemplated a nightmarish image of seven odious old men filing before him. The vision of decrepitude and degeneration passes before him in what he calls a 'cortège infernal'. The last stanza of the poem, cited above, expresses the state into which the soul is thrown after the experience. Far from the enchantment that the image of the boat had elicited in Shelley's analogy in *Prometheus Unbound*, the boat in this poem conveys the confusion of the soul. Whereas the boat in Shelley's poetry had been characterized by its light, magical character, in this poem, a heavy old boat is drawn to our attention. The soul is no longer enchanted, ethereal, magical. In Baudelaire's poem, the soul is conveyed as a heavy, degenerate entity which lacks direction, being 'without masts', and is on the verge of annihilation. The repetition of the word 'dansait' suggests the state of frenzy that the soul is in, in its descent toward the nothingness of the 'gouffre'. The poem presents an image of the soul lost in the tempest.

The poem 'Le Voyage' also offers a boat image which is identified with the soul. The nautical terminology includes mast, deck and starboard:

> Notre âme est un trois-mâts cherchant son Icarie;
> Une voix retentit sur le pont: 'Ouvre l'oeil!'
> Une voix de la hune, ardente et folle, crie:
> 'Amour ... gloire ... bonheur!' Enfer! c'est un écueil! (p. 199)

> Our soul is a three-master seeking its Icaria; a voice on deck resounds: 'Watch out!' A voice from aloft cries feverishly and madly: 'Love ... Glory ... Bliss!' O Hell! It's a reef!

In the first verse of this stanza the soul is pictured in the form of a boat aspiring toward the land of Icarus; this suggests the aspiration of the soul for flight and liberation. However, the last verse dramatically annihilates the hope expressed in the first as the boat is suddenly stopped, having hit an 'écueil' or reef. The soul is thus incapacitated, immobilized, unable to flee its vulnerable condition, just as vulnerable as a physical being. This is the exact opposite of Shelley's metaphor of the soul-boat which is liberated as it travels in exhilaration toward its paradise. In Baudelaire's poem the soul is barred from paradise, unable to escape its mortal coils.

There is also a sense of the lost soul, as can be noted in Baudelaire's poem 'Spleen LXXV'. The soul is seen wandering aimlessly in the gutters with the voice of a phantom:

> L'âme d'un vieux poète erre dans la gouttière
> Avec la triste voix d'un fantôme frileux. (p. 145)

> The soul of an old poet wanders in the gutters with the sad voice of a shivering phantom.

The soul, in this sense, is that part of man which most deeply feels solitude and aimlessness. The wandering of the soul further underlines its lack of direction, characteristic of those poems which link the soul to a non-guided boat. Even the gutter suggests water and once again evokes the purposeless journey of the poet through time.

It is most appropriate to consider Rimbaud's 'Le Bateau Ivre' (1871) in this context as an example of a further evolution of the soul-boat image to a stage of reckless journey and wreckage. Although the word 'soul' is not used, it is apparent that the boat relates to the concept most intimately and that when Rimbaud speaks of the 'bateau ivre' or the 'bateau perdu' he is referring to the disordered soul in its artistic, free, phantasmagorical, visionary escapade.

Among the images most closely connected to the boat is that of the pale flotsam ('flottaison blême') which suggests from the beginning the soul's wrecked condition:

> Et dès lors, je me suis baigné dans le Poème
> De la Mer, infusé d'astres et lactescent,
> Dévorant les azurs verts; où flottaison blême
> Et ravie, un noyé pensif parois descend . . . (p. 101)

> And from then on, I was bathed in the Poem of the Sea, fraught with stars and milky, devouring the green azure; wherein a pale and enraptured flotsam, a pensive drowned one sometimes descends . . .

The poem is a seascape: the sea is equated to the poem and is the physical region in which the soul is immersed. The plunging of the soul is expressed in concrete, physical terms and there is no mention of an abstract 'azur' or 'gouffre' as in Hugo's poems. In fact, so strong is the rebellion from the abstract that Rimbaud refers to the sea as green ('L'eau verte pénétra ma coque de sapin').

As the soul-boat proceeds recklessly in currents, in swells, striking reefs, hitting glaciers, travelling on seas which merge with skies, its itinerary is characterized by the tangible and the concrete. The physical character of the journey is stressed.

Another designation of the soul-boat is that of the drunken carcass ('carcasse ivre') which conveys its saturated state:

> Or moi, bateau perdu sous les cheveux des anses,
> Jeté par l'ouragan dans l'éther sans oiseau,
> Moi dont les Monitors et les voiliers des Hanses
> N'auraient pas repêché le carcasse ivre d'eau ... (p. 102)

> Now myself, a boat lost beneath a flock of bay, flung by the hurricane into the birdless ether, I whose Monitors and Hanseatic ships could not have retrieved the carcass drunken with water ...

In fact, the soul, as we have seen in Hugo and Baudelaire as well, has been reduced to a carcass or a deteriorated body. In the next stanza it is smoking, so completely is it destroyed. The frenzied journey of the imagination succeeds in loosening the soul. What was once considered a coherent entity is broken apart into random pieces and fragments.

So it appears that the thematic use of the boat image becomes more and more pervasive in the delineation of the soul. Other patterns such as voyage and vertigo and images such as sea and flask are subordinate to it. Sailing as it does, the boat is most prone to vacillation, movement and effects of outside forces. Tossed in turbulent waters, the boat mounts heights, sinks into depths and follows the path of wave patterns in troughs and crests.

Whereas in Shelley the soul-boat was frail, fragile, ethereal, in Baudelaire it is predominantly heavy, aged and weary. In Rimbaud, it is inebriated, moving along grotesque routes, caught in whirlpools, in disorder and chaos.

If the mutation of the soul at this particular stage of its evolution is reflected in the alternation of the soul-boat image, so the contrast between notions of soul in Shelley and Baudelaire in particular, is revealed in the alternation of the other image which is traditionally linked with the soul, i.e. the bird. Whereas in most Romantic poetry the soul has eagle wings, in Baudelaire it has the black wings of a crow. Shelley's 'Ode to Liberty', for example, conveys the rise of the soul to freedom through the image of an eagle soaring majestically:

> My soul spurned the chains of its dismay,
> And in the rapid plumes of song
> Clothed itself, sublime and strong,

(As a young eagle soars the morning clouds among,)
Hovering in verse o'er its accustomed prey.

Just as the boat image in Baudelaire is a mutation of the one in Shelley's
poetry, so also does the bird image undergo striking modifications as
manifest in Baudelaire's poem 'Brumes et Pluies':

Dans cette grande plaine où l'autan froid se joue,
Où par les longues nuits la girouette s'enroue,
Mon âme mieux qu'au temps du tiède renouveau
Ouvrira largement ses ailes de corbeau. (p. 172)

In this great plain where the cold south wind plays, where through
the long nights the weather-cock becomes hoarse, my soul, better
than in the mild climate of spring, will open wide its raven wings.

The setting is one of depression rather than of elevation. The state of
death suggested by the image of the crow permeates the poem through the
imagery of the tomb, the shroud, the 'funeral things', the darkness and
the winter setting. An eternal power of blackness here envelops the soul.

Common to the images of the soul examined in the passages above
is the overwhelming notion of the soul as the *other self*. Baudelaire
addresses his soul as a dear friend. When in 'Le Crépuscule du Soir' he
warns his soul to close its ears to the dangerous movement in the
atmosphere which will only hurt it, the poet addresses the soul with
compassion. In 'Les Sept Vieillards', the split between the self and the
soul is explicit in the fact that the poet carries on a conversation with
his soul: 'Et discutant avec mon âme déjà lasse.' In most instances
Baudelaire addresses the soul directly; he either pities it, warns it of
impending dangers or shares with it the ills of human existence. The
integrity of the soul is further stressed by the designation of particular
senses to the soul such as sight, hearing and smelling. The dichotomy
between the poet and his inner self leads us to believe that the soul is
the alter ego.[5]

The other self or alter ego which the soul frequently constitutes is
conveyed also by the existence of the soul as the subconscious. In many
instances the soul is evoked in the midst of dark tombs, alleys and
general areas of blackness, all indications of the landscape which traditionally suggests the subconscious. The most outright identification of
the soul with the subconscious is expressed in the poem entitled 'Le
Mauvais Moine':

Mon âme est un tombeau que, mauvais cénobite,
Depuis l'éternité je parcours et j'habite;
Rien n'embellit les murs de ce cloître odieux. (p. 91)

My soul is a tomb which like an evil monk I eternally traverse and
inhabit; naught adorns the walls of this odious cloister.

In this stanza, we note the dichotomy between the self ('je') and the soul. There is an objectification of the subjective; the poet projects his inner self or soul outside his person and views himself objectively. It would seem that the soul, likened to a tomb, incarnates the subconscious. The mention of the walls further suggests the closed inner region. The poem which deals with the remorse and guilt of the poet focuses on the soul or subconscious which the remorse inhabits. Another example of the soul with the subconscious can be seen in the poem 'L'Homme et la Mer' where the depth of the soul is conveyed through the alliance of the soul and the sea:

> Homme libre, toujours tu chériras la mer!
> La mer est ton miroir; tu contemples ton âme
> Dans le déroulement infini de sa lame,
> Et ton esprit n'est pas un gouffre moins amer. (p. 94)

> O free man, forever will you cherish the sea! The sea is your mirror; you contemplate your soul in the infinite unfolding of its waves, and your mind is an abyss no less painful.

The soul is associated with the darkness and infinitude triggered by the sea image. The soul, in its identification with a subterranean habitat, resembles the hidden deep regions of the subconscious. It is, moreover, the same kind of inner recess suggested in the grim image of a funeral procession in the poem 'Une Gravure Fantastique':

> Et de longs corbillards, sans tambours ni musique,
> Défilent lentement dans mon âme; l'Espoir,
> Vaincu, pleure, et l'Angoisse atroce, despotique,
> Sur mon crâne incliné plante son drapeau noir. (p. 147)

> And a long train of hearses, without drums or music, defiled slowly into my soul; Conquered Hope laments, and atrocious despotic Anguish plants its black standard on my skull which is bowed.

A related soul complex emerges in Nerval's *Aurélia* (1855) in which the same dark imagery surrounds the evocation of the soul. Though in Nerval there are no metaphors of soul *per se*, there is personification of the soul which replaces metaphoric delineation. The word conjures the ego and *alter* ego.

In the prose poem, the soul is the ego victimized by tragic destiny. The initial infliction is the death of the beloved:

> Chacun peut chercher dan ses souvenirs l'émotion la plus navrante, le coup le plus terrible frappé par le destin. (p. 359)[6]

> Each person can search his memories for the most distressing emotion, the most dreadful blow struck upon him by fate.

The subsequent activity of the soul, as described by the poet in the third section of the poem is a state of folly and extravaganza. So confused is the identity under duress that there is no longer distinction between the state of dream-madness and that of waking reality. The effect on the soul is one of doubling.

> Par un singulier effet de vibration, il me semblait que cette voix résonnait dans ma poitrine et que mon âme se rédoublait pour ainsi dire, distinctement partagée entre la vision et la réalité. (p. 364)

> By a singular effect of vibration, it appeared to me that this voice resounded in my breast and that my soul redoubled, so to speak, distinctly divided between vision and reality.

The poet is so conscious of himself that he begins to view himself objectively as we see in the eighth passage of the prose poem in which the poet-hero descends to the tomb of his beloved and identifies himself with the prince of Orient. Indeed, here is the crystallization of the *other self* which we have noticed in Baudelaire as well. Like the allegory of the 'mauvais cénobite' in the example cited above, here there is personification of the soul by the Black Orphic prince. In their allusions to the soul entrapped in the tomb in both Baudelaire and Nerval we are left with the obsessive image of an eternal mortality.

From the examination of Baudelaire's poetry, we can conclude that the mortality of the soul is more often expressed through the laden sense of its oppression than through its frustrated longing for other shores. The intoxicating images of wine and sensuality suggest only momentary transcendence and the traditional boat image of flight is doomed by obstruction. In fact, the soul in Baudelaire's imagery becomes heavy with spleen, gloom and horror as it is increasingly contaminated with the poet's mortality.

5   The Symbolists: the Failing Soul

In the poetry of the French Symbolists a major shift in the notion of the soul occurs. The duality between the soul and physical existence is totally obliterated as the soul is mired in earthly existence. For the Symbolists the soul is confined to the innermost recesses of the human consciousness. There is no redeeming chariot race, as seen in Keats, to pull the soul even temporarily out of its stagnation.[1] The soul makes no movement toward any kind of transmigration whether in dream or in the waking state. It becomes the seat of perception and the index of personality. The references to the soul in Symbolist poetry in the French language contain a descriptive factor of the poet's mood (*état d'âme*) rather than any keynote to the poet's desire to transcend the human condition. This pattern is inherent in the soul metaphors discovered particularly in the writings of Verlaine, Maeterlinck and Mallarmé and illustrated obsessively in the Symbolist coterie of poets.

In describing the tonality of the *soul* in Verlaine, Guy Michaud in his *Message Poétique du Symbolisme* observes a distinction between the Romantic soul, the focus of the affective expression, and the soul as it emanates in Symbolist writings, fragile, indescribable, ineffable, emotionally muted. Michaud further declares that the very objective of Symbolist poetry is to express this sense of soul which is pervasive and ephemeral at the same time. He writes:

> Etre soi, c'est plus encore que toute autre chose, trouver et exprimer son âme. Non l'âme des Romantiques, cette sentimentalité grossière de filles publiques, qui s'exhale en lieux communs et en thèmes galvaudés ... L'âme, c'est quelque chose d'insaisissable, des nuances, des émotions, des sensations, moins que cela encore: une atmosphère, une tonalité, une teinte proprement indicible.[2]

> To be oneself, is, more than anything else, to find and express one's soul. Not the soul of the Romantics, that gross sentimentality of prostitutes which issues forth in common places and in unbridled themes ... The soul is something unseizable – nuances, emotions, sensations, even less specific than that: an atmosphere, a tonality, a shade which appropriately is undefined.

Michaud does not elaborate on the distinction he notes; he does not say how this uncertain and fragile character of the soul affects the imagery of the poetry. We have indeed a situation here where it is no longer the movements of the soul and the direction of these movements that are the chief concern, but rather the state or condition of the soul. In Symbolist poetry, the excessive usage of the expression 'état d'âme' finally destroys its literal character and makes it synonymous with 'mood', which is representative of the splenetic state of the soul. The 'état d'âme', which is the focus of the subjectivity of the Symbolist poet, suggests that the soul has assumed the deplorable character of the human condition. The soul has settled into an exitless state. The interpretation of 'état d'âme' as 'mood' does not take into consideration the outright alliance of soul and state. The state measures the soul's confinement according to spatio-temporal limits. Whereas in Baudelaire the soul is drawn in two opposing directions, vacillating and shifting momentarily, in the Symbolists the soul emerges as a static entity upon which the elements act, causing erosion and deterioration. But there is generally no apparent justification for ageing and disease, symptomatic of the whole decadent climate of the time. The soul, detached from the notion of a happier past and from the promise of a compensating future, remains to be observed in its meagre present state.

Actually the notion of the state of the soul is the poetic parallel, it seems to me, of the phenomenological notion of *Dasein*. The poetry we are examining is also cast in the context of phenomena. As the ineluctable centre of human existence the soul is surrounded by landscapes.

When we examine individual poems, however, we can observe the variations of landscape which convey the states of the soul. A striking example is Verlaine's poem, 'Clair de Lune'. In this poem, the soul is projected into nature and is incorporated with a landscape portrait of the soul. Referring to his loved one, Verlaine describes her in terms of a physical setting:

Votre âme est un paysage choisi
Que vont charmant masques et bergamasques
Jouant du luth et dansant et quasi
Tristes sous leurs déguisements fantasques.

Tout en chantant sur le mode mineur
L'amour vainqueur et la vie opportune,
Ils n'ont pas l'air de croire à leur bonheur
Et leur chanson se mêle au clair de lune,

Au calme clair de lune triste et beau,
Qui fait rêver les oiseaux dans les arbres
Et sangloter d'extase les jets d'eau,
Les grands jets d'eau sveltes parmi les marbres. (p. 83)[8]

Your soul is a choice landscape charmed by masques and berga-masques playing the lute and dancing and seeming sad under their strange disguises. While singing in their minor mode of triumphant love and fortunate life, they do not seem to believe in their bliss, and their song mingles with the moonlight. With the calm moonlight that is sad and beautiful, that makes the birds dream in the trees and makes the fountains sob in ecstasy, those grand smooth fountains amidst the marble.

In this poem, the soul's melancholy has a character of ambivalence, which is evoked by the mingling of images of gaiety and sadness. The ineffability of the mood is conveyed by the nuances of physical nature, in the frame of a garden in moonlight. The soul appeals, as an objectified scene, to several senses at once: the visual, the auditory, and the kinetic with the interplay of dance, instruments and light. Instead of describing the soul directly with adjectives appropriate to it, the poet intimates the indescribable quality of the soul by the juxtaposition in the scene itself of varying attributes ranging from the melancholy of the minor music to the gaiety of the dance, from the liquid of the water-spouts to the solid of the marble.

In another instance, in the first poem of 'Ariettes Oubliées' in *Romances Sans Paroles*, the soul is cast onto a plain, permeating it with lamentations:

Cette âme qui se lamente
En cette plaine dormante
C'est la nôtre, n'est-ce pas?
La mienne, dis, et la tienne,
Dont s'exhale l'humble antienne
Par ce tiède soir, tout bas? (p. 121)

This soul, which laments in this sleeping plain, is ours. Is that not so? It is mine, right? and yours whose humble hymn breathes into the warm eventide.

The plain, in fact, which is characterized by a dull monotony in 'Ariettes Oubliées: VII', is the physical correlative of the soul's boredom:

Dans l'interminable
Ennui da la plaine
La neige incertaine
Luit comme du sable. (p. 125)

In the interminable boredom of the plain, the uncertain snow shines like sand.

The outstanding frequency of the word in Verlaine's poetry indicates, it would seem to me, that the word 'soul' can be replaced by 'I' or the ego, as it becomes the focus of consciousness, intervening between the senses and the reason, or the senses and the heart. The soul is the seat of sensibilities. It trembles and is surprised as in the poem 'Les Ingénus':

> Le soir tombait, un soir équivoque d'automne:
> Les belles, se pendant rêveuses à nos bras,
> Dirent alors des mots si spécieux, tout bas,
> Que notre âme, depuis ce temps, tremble et s'étonne. (p. 86)

Night fell, an ambiguous autumn evening: the belles hanging dreamy on our arms, did utter such special words, so softly, that since then our soul trembles and wonders in surprise.

It radiates, as evidenced in the poem entitled 'Initium', where the soul of the beloved generates rays and ingrains passion in the poet:

> Cependant elle allait, et la mazurque lente,
> La portait dan son rhythme indolent comme un vers,
>   Rime mélodieuse, image étincelante,
> Et son âme d'enfant rayonnait à travers
> La sensuelle ampleur de ses yeux gris et verts. (p. 62)

Meanwhile she was going on, and the slow mazurka carried her in its listless rhythm like a verse: a melodious rhyme, a glistening image. And her childlike soul was radiating through the sensual fullness of her grey-green eyes.

The soul vibrates as well in, for example, the poem 'Nocturne Parisien':

> Il brame un de ces airs, romances ou polkas,
> Qu'enfants nous tapotions sur nos harmonicas
> Et qui font, lents ou vifs, réjouissants ou tristes,
> Vibrer l'âme aux proscrits, aux femmes, aux artistes. (p. 69)

He utters one of those airs of romances or polkas which as children we would strum on our harmonicas and which, slowly or lively, cheerfully or sadly, make the soul vibrate to outcasts, women, and artists.

In the poem 'Ariettes Oubliées: 1,' the soul laments ('cette âme qui se lamente') in a state of utter affliction. Even more violent sensations are attributed to the soul. In 'Langueur', Verlaine blatently proclaims the state of decadence with which he identifies himself; the soul suffers an acute physical sensation of nausea:

> Je suis l'Empire à la fin de la décadence, . . .
> L'âme seulette a mal au coeur d'un ennui dense. (p. 250)

> I am the Empire at the close of decadence, ... The lone soul is sickened from a dense boredom.

This is an obvious allusion in contrast to Baudelaire's evocation of the same mood. In many of his poems, Baudelaire related his ennui to the environment that provoked it. In Verlaine, the soul is not moving toward ennui, it is already there at the beginning of the poem. Verlaine's nausea ('mal au coeur') is the existentialist metaphor for the total boredom and purposelessness that engulf the poet. The physical ailment of the soul is an indication of the degree of the invasion of the nausea. In addition, the soul goes so far as finally to die in 'Amour III', a poem which is an invective against women as the cause of death:

> O la femme! Prudent, sage, calme ennemi ...
> Et parfois induit le dormeur en telle mort
> Délicieuse par quoi l'âme meurt aussi! (p. 318)

> O Woman! Prudent, wise, and calm enemy ... and sometimes leads the sleeper into so delicious a death, in which the soul dies as well.

Indeed the panorama of sensations is vast and the soul suffers in a variety of ways which stress its human characteristic of vulnerability.

In the following passage, taken from the poem 'Crépuscule du Soir Mystique', the soul, situated between the senses and reason, as a distinct identity, links the two in a mutual engulfment by memory:

> De parfums lourds et chauds, dont le poison
>   Dahlia, lys, tulipe et renoncule
> Noyant mes sens, mon âme et ma raison,
> Mêle, dans une immense pâmoison,
> Le Souvenir avec le Crépuscule. (p. 54)

> Heavy and warm fragrances, whose poison of dahlia, lily, tulip and buttercup drowning my senses, my soul and my reason, is blending Memory with Twilight in a vast swoon.

Sometimes, the soul produces synaesthesia as, for example, in the poem 'Nocturne Parisien':

> Et dans une harmonie étrange et fantastique
> Qui tient de la musique et tient de la plastique,
> L'âme, les inondant de lumière et de chant,
> Mêle les sons de l'orgue aux rayons du couchant. (p. 69)

> And in a strange and fanciful harmony which proceeds from music and from the plastic power, the soul, flooding them with light and song, blends the sounds of the organ with the rays of the setting sun.

Sometimes, the soul takes part in a dialogue with the heart, as witnessed in the fanciful poem 'Ariettes Oubliées: VII' of *Romances Sans Paroles*:

O triste, triste était mon âme
A cause, à cause d'une femme . . .

Mon âme dit à mon coeur: Sais-je
Moi-même, que nous vent ce piège . . . (p 125)

O sad, sad was my soul because, because of a woman . . . My soul speaks to my heart: Do I know myself what this snare means to us . . .

The soul is a breath, it is an auxiliary power of the mind, evident, for example, in the phrase 'mon âme et ma raison' from 'Crépuscule du Soir Mystique'; it is an auxiliary power of the heart as revealed, for instance, in 'Ariettes Oubliées: II': 'mon âme et mon coeur en délires.' It is even expressed as a collective psyche, particularly as it links dear ones in empathy:

Nous sommes en des temps infâmes
Ou le marrage des âmes
Doit sceller l'union des coeurs[4]

We are in infamous times wherein the marriage of souls ought to seal the union of hearts.

and also as the plural possessive adjective *notre* ('notre âme, depuis ce temps, tremble et s'étonne'[5]) and the plural possessive pronoun *la nôtre* ('cette âme qui se lamente . . . c'est la nôtre'[6]) are used with it.

As we proceed in our examination from Verlaine to Mallarmé and the poets of the Symbolist school, we note certain recurring patterns which designations of the soul assume. On the one hand, there is the abstract entity of the void ('le néant') invading the soul in Mallarmé's poetry, on the other hand there are the vivid clichés which depict the soul in the poetry of the Symbolist group. The titles of collections of Symbolist poetry such as René Ghil's *Légendes d'Ames et de Sang*, Jean Lorrain's *Ames d'Automne* and Stuart Merrill's 'Ame d'Automne', in *Petits Poèmes d'Automne* are clear evidence of the excessive preoccupation with the soul in this period.

Calcification and vacuity are characteristic of Mallarmé's designation of the soul. A hardened soul, for example, figures in the poem 'Les Fenêtres' (1863) and relates most closely to the metaphysical condition of the poet: his inability to transcend the mortal state conveyed in terms of a hospital scene. The sickly soul has sordid, earthly appetites:

Ainsi, pris du dégoût de l'homme à l'âme dure
Vautré dans le bonheur, où ses seuls appétits
Mangent, et qui s'entête à chercher cette ordure
Pour l'offrir à la femme allaitant ses petits. (p. 33)[7]

Thus, disgusted with man of a hard soul wallowing in happiness, whose sole cravings satisfy themselves, and who is obstinately seeking that ordure to present it to some woman nursing her little ones.

When the poet attempts to change this image of the soul and turns to the 'azure' heights, it is in vain. The soul does not have access to the windows of eternity. The hardened image of the soul remains the characteristic one. There is the resignation of the earthly scene: 'Mais, hélas! Ici-bas est maître'. In fact, the soul is hardened to a state of insensibility and relates most closely to the condition of matter as indicated in the lines from the poem 'L'Azur' (1864):

Le Ciel est mort. Vers toi, j'accours! donne, ô matière,
L'oubli de l'Idéal cruel et du Péché
A ce martyr qui vient partager la litière
Où le bétail heureux des hommes est couché. (p. 38)

Heaven is dead. Towards you I hasten! O matter, grant forgetfulness of the cruel Ideal and of Sin to this martyr who comes to share the litter where the contented cattle of men lie.

Exiled and martyred, the soul resides in the habitat of the earth with a finality which precludes possibility of migration.

Mallarmé's 'L'Azur' depicts the soul as an outcast of the 'azure' heights. The soul is rendered vacant and empty in its condition on land. The emphasis is upon the inability of the soul to flee:

Fuyant, les yeux fermés, je le sens qui regarde
Avec l'intensité d'un remords atterrant,
Mon âme vide. Où fuir? Et quelle nuit hagarde
Jeter, lambeaux, jeter sur ce mépris navrant? (p. 37)

Fleeing, with closed eyes, I feel it looking with the intensity of an overwhelming remorse upon my empty soul. Where to flee? And what wild night should I thrust, tattered as I am, upon this harrowing scorn?

Though no actual soul metaphors exist, the stifling, suffocating aspect of the soul's state is conveyed through the pervasive image of the heavy ceiling of fog and mist which blocks the blue 'azure' of eternity:

Brouillards, montez! Versez vos cendres monotones
Avec de longs haillons de brume dans les cieux
Qui noiera le marais livide des automnes
Et bâtissez un grand plafond silencieux!

Mists, ascend! Pour forth your monotonous embers with long rags of fog into the skies which will drown the livid marsh of autumns and will create a silent ceiling.

The emptiness of silence confronts the soul and is the equivalent on the auditory level of the spatial void. Additional images of soot, smoke and setting suns emerge in the poem as correlatives of the soul's state.

In particular, the 'jet d'eau', one of the most commonplace images in the Symbolist school, is illustrative of the futility of the soul's longing. Mallarmé's 'Soupir' (1864) succinctly underlines its frustrated condition:

> Mon âme vers ton front où rêve, ô calme soeur,
> Un automne jonché de taches de rousseur,
> Et vers le ciel errant de ton oeil angélique
> Monte, comme dans un jardin mélancolique,
> Fidèle, un blanc jet d'eau soupire vers l'Azur!
>   Vers l'Azur attendri d'Octobre pâle et pur
> Qui mire aux grands bassins sa langueur infinie
> Et laisse, sur l'eau morte où la fauve agonie
> Des feuilles erre au vent et creuse un froid sillon,
> Se traîner le soleil jaune d'un long rayon. (p. 39)

My soul, towards your brow, o calm sister, where a freckled autumn dreams, and towards the lost sky of your angelic eye, ascends like the faithful clear waters of the fountain sigh for the azure. Towards the azure mellowed by the pale and pure October which reflects in large basins its infinite languor and lets the yellow sun plough a cold track with a long ray upon the dead waters where the tawny agony of leaves rambles in the wind.

An autumnal setting, a melancholy garden, and dead waters are the landscape of the soul. The trajectory of the waters from the fountain is the most graphic representation of the soul's futile attempt at transcendence. Sterility is the characteristic of the large basins containing dead waters. Where Mallarmé mentions the empty soul (l'âme vide') in the poem 'L'Azur', he intimates it in the poem 'Soupir' through images which replace the word and function as metonymy.

The Symbolist soul-imagery which is profuse in the period to follow serves to emphasize certain characteristics which the soul readily assumes in the waning years of the century. Where Mallarmé employs the word infrequently, the Symbolists, who form a literary school, use the word excessively and transform the original metaphors into standard, conventional ones. The mediocre poets assimilate the metaphors and in their overuse of them they develop clichés. In this respect, they are important in providing clear examples of the evolution of the word-concept at this state of its development. What remains subtle in a greater poet, is obvious in a lesser one. The lesser poet reveals rather than conceals the soul's meaning which serves as representative of a state of sensibility germane to the era.

It is in this light that we examine the following poem typical of the time. Heavily laden with soul-images is Albert Samain's 'Mon Ame est une infante en robe de parade', from *Au Jardin de l'Infante* (1893). The poem contains many of the key symbols used by the Symbolists as they convey the tonality of the soul. Composed of eleven stanzas, the poem offers an extended metaphor of the soul. The soul is personified as an infanta and keeps the feminine gender which the word commands in the French language:

Mon Ame est une infante en robe de parade,
Dont l'exil se reflète, éternel et royal,
Aux grands miroirs déserts d'un vieil Escurial
Ainsi qu'une galère oubliée en la rade . . .

Elle est là résignée, et douce, et sans surprise,
Sachant trop pour lutter comme tout est fatal,
Et se sentant, malgré quelque dédain fatal,
Sensible à la pitié comme l'onde à la brise.

Elle est là résignée, et douce en ses sanglots,
Plus sombre seulement quand elle évoque en songe
Quelque Armade sombrée à l'éternel mensonge,
Et tant de beaux espoirs endormis sous les flots . . .

Les vieux mirages d'or ont dissipé son deuil,
Et, dans les visions où son ennui s'échappe,
Soudain – gloire ou soleil – un rayon qui la frappe
Allume en elle tous les rubis de l'orgueil.

Mais d'un sourire triste elle apaise ces fièvres;
Et, redoutant la foule aux tumultes de fer,
Elle écoute la vie – au loin – comme la mer . . .
Et le secret se fait plus profond sur ses lèvres.

Rien n'émeut d'un frisson l'eau pâle de ses yeux,
Où s'est assis l'Esprit voilé des Villes mortes;
Et par les salles, où sans bruit tournent les portes,
Elle va, s'enchantant de mots mystérieux.

L'eau vaine des jets d'eau là-bas tombe en cascade,
Et, pâle à la croisée, une tulipe aux doigts,
Elle est là, reflétée aux miroirs d'autrefois,
Ainsi qu'une galère oubliée en la rade.

Mon Ame est une infante en robe de parade. (pp. 8–10)[8]

My soul is an infanta in stately dress, whose exile, eternal and royal, is reflected in the large vacant mirrors of an old Escurial like a galley forgotten in the roads. She is there, resigned, sweet and sans surprise, knowing too much to struggle since all is deemed fatal, and feeling moved, despite some fatal scorn, by pity as the wave by the breeze. She is there, resigned, sweet in her sobbing, only more sombre when she evokes in dream some Armada drowned by the eternal illusion, and so many beautiful hopes laid to sleep under the waters. The old mirages of gold dispelled her mourning, and, in the visions wherein her troubles vanish, suddenly a ray of glory or of sunlight striking her kindles all the rubies of pride. But with a sad smile she appeases these fevers, and dreading the crowd with its harsh uproar she listens to life – in the distance – like the sea. And the secret grows deeper under her lips. Nothing moves as much as a ripple the pale water of her eyes where the veiled ghost of dead cities is seated; and through the halls in which the doors move noiselessly she goes, delighting herself with mysterious words. Vainly do the fountain waters thither fall in cascades. And pale, at the casement, a tulip in her fingers, she is there, reflected in the mirrors of yore, like a galley forgotten in the roads. My soul is an infanta in stately dress.

The metaphor of the infanta cloistered in the forgotten demesne of Escurial is suggestive of various attributes of the soul. First and foremost the sense of the obsolete condition of the soul is conveyed. The infanta belongs to another age. She remains hidden and removed in the palace of Escurial which has lost the splendour of its past. The woman and the era from which she stems are superannuated: the correlative of the obsolete soul. The image of the empty mirrors are particularly significant in stressing the vacancy of the soul. In peering into them, the infanta only discovers the emptiness of her own alter-ego. Her attempt to flee this desolate condition is thwarted. Although she is momentarily allured by dreams and enchantment with promise of flight to new horizons, she is resigned to the fatal condition of the static, immobile Escurial. The reference to the Armada evokes at once the glory and defeat of Spain. There is the image of the shipwreck of hope in the lines concerning the drowning of the Armada:

> Quelque Armade sombrée à l'éternel mensonge,
> Et tant de beaux espoirs endormis sous les flots.

'Sombrée' refers to the drowning and 'flots' suggests the seascape which is the scene of the disaster. But as the poem nears its end, more static images are linked with the soul. Pale waters and garden fountains are images of a soul which has become emotionally muted. Veiled cities, shadowy waters of dead canals, useless spurts of water from placid fountains suggest the stagnation of the soul's state.

One of the major images of the poem, the old, ignoble ship which is desolate and abandoned is a striking instance of the state of soul at the end of the century:

Elle est là, reflétée aux miroirs d'autrefois,
Ainsi qu'une galère oubliée en la rade.

Once again the soul-boat looms as the major image. Its condition has become firmly set in terms of the heavy, freighted ship cast away, forgotten and forsaken. It is a further evolution of Baudelaire's image of the old barge or 'vieille gabarre' signalled earlier in this study. But where in Baudelaire, emphasis was placed upon the struggle of the ship, here attention is focused upon the quiet resignation apparent in the soul-boat which is docked and standing. There is irony in the reduction of the noble infanta to the ignoble ship. Indeed, the juxtaposition of the two images is an ironic poetic statement concerning the soul's state. Like the soul, the infanta has survived her stature and therefore her significance.

In the fourth poem from the series, 'L'Allée Solitaire', also in Samain's *Au Jardin de l'Infante*, the metaphor of the ancient manor shut from the outer world is another clear image of the soul:

Vague et noyée au fond du brouillard hiémal,
Mon âme est un manoir dont les vitres sont closes,
Ce soir, l'ennui visqueux suinte au long des choses
Et je titube au mur obscur de l'animal. (p. 163)

Faint and drowned in the depths of a wintry fog, my soul is a manor whose windows are closed. This evening the viscous boredom oozes from things at large and I stagger to the dark inhuman wall.

The wintry fog envelops the manor as the 'ennui' or boredom penetrates the structure of self. The closed windows mark the complete shift to the interior. The soul becomes clearly here the alter ego and the feminine gender of the soul creates an androgynous complexity for the narcissistic contemplation of self.

In Jean Moreas' 'Conte d'Amour' of the collection of poems *Les Syrtes* (1884) we encounter another use of the manor image to designate the soul:

Mon coeur est un cercueil vide dans une tombe;
Mon âme est un manoir hanté par les corbeaux.[9]

My heart is an empty coffin in a tomb. My soul is a manor haunted by crows.

The blackness of the crows invades the soul. The dream sequence in which this metaphor appears offers no transcendence; rather it is revealed in terms of a low ceiling of the sky.

In Stuart Merrill's *Petits Poèmes d'Automne* (1887–97) clichés of withered flowers and dying swans go beyond metaphor and become metonymy in depicting the soul's steady deterioration. The soul is cast in autumnal settings as the title of a section of the poems, 'Ame d'Automne', indicates. Take the overt image of the dying rose:

Mon âme, en une rose,
Est morte de douleur:
C'est l'histoire morose
Du rêve et de la fleur . . .

Voici le vent d'automne
Sur mon âme et les fleurs;
Et pourtant je m'étonne
De tout ce ciel en pleurs.

O rose de mon rêve,
Fleuriras-tu jamais?
Naîtras-tu de sa sève,
Amour, aux futurs Mais? (p. 149)[10]

My soul, in a rose, is dead of sorrow. It's the morose story of the dream and the flower. Here is the autumn wind on my soul and on the flowers; and yet I wonder at this whole sky in tears. O rose of my dream, will you never bloom? Will you be born of its sap, love, in the Mays of the future?

Or the image of the dying swan:

O Passantes, faites le signe,
Du pardon et de l'infortune
Sur l'âme qui meurt comme un cygne
Blessé par l'archer de la lune. (p. 159)

O passers-by, make the sign of pardon and of misfortune on the soul that dies like a swan wounded by the bow of the moon.

Images of the dying soul are multiplied as we approach the end of the century and forecast the dead souls in the next and final period in the evolution of the word-concept. The examples above contain key images of the birds and boats of earlier lyrics. There is also the metonymy of the dying phantom in Merrill's *Hantise* in *Les Gammes* (1887):

Par les vastes forêts, à l'heure vespérale,
Les ruisseaux endormeurs modulent leurs sanglots;
Mon âme s'alanguit d'une horreur sépulcrale
A l'heure vespérale où murmurent les flots.

Les ruisseaux endormeurs modulent leurs sanglots
Sous les feuilles que frôle un vent crépusculaire;
A l'heure vespérale où murmurent les flots
Un fantôme s'effare en l'ombre funéraire.

Sous les feuilles que frôle un vent crépusculaire
La pâleur de la lune illumine le soir:
Un fantôme s'effare en l'ombre funéraire
Et l'âme de l'air râle en brumes d'encensoir

La pâleur de la lune illumine le soir,
Impalpable remous de la marée astrale,
Et l'âme de l'air râle en brumes d'encensoir
Par les vastes forêts, à l'heure vespérale. (p. 30)

In the vast forests at the hour of vespers, the lulling streams modulate their sobbing; my soul languishes from sepulchral horror at the hour of vespers when the waves murmur. The lulling streams modulate their sobbing amidst the leaves rustled by wind at twilight; at the hour of vespers when the waves murmur, a phantom is affright in the funereal shades. Amidst the leaves rustled by wind at twilight, the lunar pallor illuminates the evening: a phantom is affright in the funereal shades and the soul of the air rattles in mists from the censer. The lunar pallor illuminates the evening, an impalpable eddy of the astral tide, and the soul of the air rattles in mists from the censer in the vast forests at the hour of vespers.

In the first stanza the soul is evoked in the autumnal setting. The hour of vespers suggests the waning of the soul. The soul withers like flowers, as the word 's'alanguit' suggests. As we reach the second stanza, it becomes clear that the soul is replaced by the phantom image, its metonymy. An entire complex of images relate to the soul-phantom: the rustling leaves, the twilight, the pale moon, the receptacle of incense. The mingling of auditory, visual and olfactory images contribute to depict the soul's state.

From the personal soul we move to the universal soul as the soul is described in terms of a general atmosphere. The universal soul, a reflection of the individual soul, is evoked:

Et l'âme de l'air râle en brumes d'encensoir.

The same occurs in Jules Laforgue's 'Nobles et Touchantes Divagations sous la Lune':

Un chien perdu grelotte en abois à la Lune . . .
Oh, pourquoi ce sanglot quand nul ne l'a battu?
Et nuits! que partout la même Ame! En est-il une
Qui n'aboie à l'Exil ainsi qu'un chien perdu? (p. 214)[11]

A lost dog trembles as it barks at the moon . . . O! Why this sobbing when no one has struck him? And nights! How the same soul is everywhere! Is there not one that barks not in exile like a lost dog?

The soul-dog of the above passage is associated with the human soul in their common alienation and exile. It is to be noted that where in Wordsworth the universal soul strengthened the particular, fortified and nurtured it, in these later instances the soul makes the dying more insurmountable. A denial of the vital sense of soul is evident in the shift of the soul from the life force to the death rattle.

We find a dramatic instance of the dying figure of the soul in the image of the shrouded cadaver of Jean Lorrain's 'Comme un Lointain Etang':

Comme un lointain étang baigné de clair de lune,
Le passé m'apparaît dans l'ombre de l'oubli,
Mon âme, entre les joncs, cadavre enseveli.
S'y corrompt lentement dans l'eau saumâtre et brune.

Les croyances d'antan s'effritent une à une,
Tandis qu'à l'horizon suavement pâli,
Un vague appel de cor, un murmure affaibli
Fait vibrer le silence endormi sur la dune.

O pâle vision, étang crépusculaire,
Dors en paix! pleure en vain, olifant légendaire,
O nostalgique écho des étés révolus!

Un trou saignant au front, les esperances fées,
De longs glaïeuls flétris et de lys morts coiffées,
Au son charmeur du cor ne s'éveilleront plus.[12]

Like a faraway pond bathed in moonlight, the past appears to me in the shadow of forgetfulness. My soul amongst the rush, a shrouded cadaver, decays there slowly in the brown and brackish water. The beliefs of yesteryear wane one by one while at the horizon gently fainting, a vague call of the horn, a weakened murmur, makes the sleeping silence reverberate on the dune. O faint vision, pond of twilight, sleep in peace! Cry in vain, legendary horn of ivory, O nostalgic echo of ending summers! A bleeding hole on the brow, the hopes of fairies, long withered gladioli and dead lilies well groomed, will no longer awaken to the enchanting sound of the horn.

The substitution of the cadaver for the soul has occurred in this poem and prefigures a whole trend of such metaphors yet to be observed. Like the corpse, the soul undergoes deterioration in a scene marked by typical decadent imagery of brackish water, dead flowers and fog. Futility is everywhere apparent, especially vivid in the frequent reference to the horns which attempt to resurrect the past and the ironic echo of silence which returns.

This type of image is strikingly present in the nihilistic poetry of Laforgue for whom both body and soul were located in a background of attrition and decay. The soul undergoes a process of fermentation in Laforgue's 'Complainte du Pauvre Jeune Homme' (1887):

> Quand ce jeune homme rentra chez lui,
> Quand ce jeune homme rentra chez lui,
> Il mit le nez dans sa belle âme,
> Ou fermentaient des tas d'ennuis!
>   Ame,
>   Ma belle âme,
> Leur huile est trop sal' pour ta flamme! (p. 125)

When the young man returned home, when the young man returned home, he stuck his nose into his gentle soul where a heap of boredoms were fermenting! Soul, my gentle soul, their oils are too sordid for your flame!

The metaphysical 'ennui' receives the concrete designation of fermentation as it attacks the soul and destroys it. The attrition is suggested in the transformation of the pure ('flamme') to the sordid ('sal'). The evocation of the useless dikes and grim funeral procession are the sign for the inevitable devastation of the soul:

> Quand les croq'morts vinrent chez lui,
> Quand les croq'morts vinrent chez lui,
> Ils virent qu' c'était un' belle âme,
> Comme on n'en fait plus aujourd'hui!
>   Ame,
>   Dors, belle âme,
> Quand on est mort c'est pour de bon. (p. 126)

When the undertakers called, when the undertakers called, they saw that it was a gentle soul, like they don't make these days. Soul, sleep, gentle soul. When one is dead, it's for good.

But if Laforgue has to evoke the aridity of the moon to convey the decadence of the soul, other poets revert to Baudelaire's urban landscapes to demonstrate the soul's steady degeneration. Verhaeren's 'Londres' (1896) is an example:

> Et ce Londres de fonte et de bronze, mon âme,
> Où des plaques de fer claquent sous des hangars,
>   Où des voiles s'en vont, sans Notre-Dame
> Pour étoile, s'en vont, là-bas, vers les hasards.
>
> Gares de suie et de fumée, où du gaz pleure
> Ses spleens d'argent lointain vers des chemin d'éclair
>   Où des bêtes d'ennui bâillent à l'heure
> Dolente immensement, qui tinte à Westminster.

Et ces quais infinis de lanternes fatales,
Parques dont les fuseaux plongent aux profondeurs,
　Et ces marins noyés, sous les pétales
Des fleurs de boue où la flamme met des lueurs.

Et ces châles et ces gestes de femmes soûles,
Et ces alcools de lettres d'or jusques aux toits,
　Et ce tout à coup la mort, parmi ces foules;
O mon âme du soir, ce Londres noir qui traine en toi![13]

And this London of iron and of bronze, my soul, where plates of
steel clack under the hangars, where sails set forth without the Holy
Virgin as guiding star, setting forth for the perils of the sea. Railway
stations of soot and of smoke, where gas sheds tears of silver spleen
into the distance towards the lighted passageways, where beasts of
boredom yawn at the immensely doleful hour which tolls at Westminster. And these endless wharves with fateful lighting, Fates
whose spindles reach into the depths, and these drowned seamen
under the petals of mud-flowers where the light glimmers. And these
shawls and gestures of drunken women, and these quintessences
of golden letters at the roofs, and suddenly death, amongst the
crowds: O my soul of the evening with black London trailing in
you!

We have only to point to the series of sordid images which compose the
landscape: the slabs of iron ('plaques der fer'), the soot ('suie'), the gas
('gaz'), the mud ('boue'). The soul is contaminated in its exposure to
the sordidness, and steadily assumes its character. Humanity is represented in the drowned sailors, the drunken women and the crowds. The
tone is the plaintive toll of the Westminster bells. The urban scene is
the anatomy of the sordid soul.

In fine, the various images assigned to the soul in the poetry of the
Symbolist school point to its stifling condition, its exile, enclosure,
sordidness and general obsolete status. In observing a major figure like
Maeterlinck, we shall note that many of these images recur in less
stereotype character.

When we come to Maeterlinck the soul-self becomes the subject of
philosophical meditations and the word 'soul' is used in the poetry with
deliberate rather than spontaneous connotation as it is evident in most
of the poetry previously examined. In the essay 'Le Silence'[14] there is
a constant concern with inter-soul communication through silence, and
in the discussion of this kind of relationship between souls Maeterlinck
reveals the fact that for him soul is the primal self unconstrained by
language. Indeed when in another article entitled 'L'Immortalité' he
talks of the self or ego, the meaning is conveyed in the same terms as for
the soul. He gropes for a definition and questions its scope:

Quel sera l'état de ce moi, de ce foyer central, réceptacle de toutes
nos sensations, lieu où converge tout ce qui appartient en propre à
notre vie, point suprême, point 'égotique' de notre être, si l'on peut
hasarder ce néologisme?[15]

What will be the state of this self, of this central hall, receptacle of
all our sensations, place where converges all that belongs exclusively
to our life, supreme point, that point of our being which is 'égotique',
if we can run the risk of such a neologism?

In his search for a definition of this intangible but very real sense of
soul he circumvents it, and is better able to say what it isn't than what
it is.

The reason that the articles have a pertinence to our study is that
Maeterlinck's circumlocutions about soul and self emerge in poetic
imagery that is extensively permeated with the notion of soul. Almost
every poem in his collection of poems called *Serres Chaudes* refers to
the soul and its susceptibilities. The soul has an anatomy including lips,
fingers, breath and hands as illustrated in the poem 'Aquarium':

Hélas! mes voeux n'amènent plus
Mon âme aux rives des paupières,
Elle est descendue au reflux
    De ses prières.

Elle est au fond de mes yeux clos,
Et seule son haleine lasse
Elève encore à fleur des eaux,
    Ses lys de glace.

Ses lèvres au fond des douleurs,
Semblent closes à mille lieues,
Et je les voix chanter des fleurs
    A tiges bleues.

Ses doigts blanchissent mes regards,
En suivant la trace incolore
De ses lys à jamais épars
    Et morts d'éclore.

Et je sais qu'elle doit mourir
En joignant ses mains impuissantes,
Et lasses enfin de cueillir
    Ces fleurs absentes. (pp. 61–2)[16]

Alas! My desires no longer lead my soul to the banks of the eyelids,
it has descended into the flux of its entreaties. It is in the depths of
my closed eyes, and only its weary breath still raises its listless lilies
to the level of the waters. Its lips in the depths of sorrows seem

closed in thousands of places, and I see them singing of flowers with blue stems. Its fingers make my glances blank, following the colourless trace of its lilies forever scattered and dead from blooming. And I know that it must die joining together its impotent hands weary at last of gathering these missing flowers.

The hands recur frequently and generally convey inaction and frustration, as in the poem 'Oraison':

Mon âme est pâle d'impuissance
Et de blanches inactions.

Mon âme aux oeuvres délaissées,
Mon âme pâle de sanglots
Regarde en vain ses mains lassées
Trembler à fleur de l'inéclos. (p. 9)

My soul is pale with impotence and with white inactions. My soul of abandoned works, my soul pale with sobbing vainly watches her wearied hands tremble with the budded flower.

Sickness is inflicted on the soul as well, explicitly conveyed in the poem 'Chasses Lasses':

Mon âme est malade aujourd'hui
Mon âme est malade d'absences,
Mon âme a le mal des silences. (p. 33)

My soul is sick today. My soul is sick of absences. My soul has the sickness of silences.

The soul is 'sick of absence', and has the 'sickness of silence'. Both these expressions point once again to the incapacity of the soul to either nurture itself or to express itself. Indeed the soul is characterized as impotent. Weariness is one of the conditions most frequently attributed to the soul: *indolente* and *lasse* are the most frequent adjectives associated with *âme*. In 'Visions', for example, the poet evokes his 'âme indolente' which suffers from extreme 'ennui':

Et lent sur mon âme indolente,
L'ennui de ces vagues amours
Luire immobile et pour toujours,
Comme une lune pâle et lente. (p. 68)

And slowly upon my indolent soul, the ennui of these uncertain loves shines motionless and forevermore like a pale and late-risen moon.

The poem 'Ame de Nuit' offers a striking example in which the poet uses the word *lasse* repeatedly to define the soul:

Mon âme en est triste à la fin;
Elle est triste enfin d'être lasse;
Elle est lasse enfin d'être en vain;
Elle est triste et lasse à la fin. (p. 89)

In the end my soul is saddened by it. It is at last sad of being weary.
It is weary at last of being in vain; it is sad and weary in the end.

In addition, anguish seizes the soul and overwhelms it, as expressed in
the poem 'Oraison': 'Mon âme a peur comme une femme' (p. 37).

Finally the soul is trapped, suffocating in an airtight enclosure under
glass ('mon âme enclose sous verre'[17]) as the title explicitly indicates:
Serres Chaudes. The pervasive image of the hothouse comes to represent the soul's condition: stifling, trapped ('mon âme au piège'[18]),
sweating ('âme chaude', 'âme humide'[19]), leading an artificial existence, separated from nature, isolated as if in a vacuum. There is, in
fact, no longer any alliance with nature; nature is indifferent to the
soul and does not infuse it with vitality. No panacea is foreseen for the
soul in its eternal frustration.

These bits and pieces of soul-imagery conveying the fragmentation
of the soul are significant indices of the strain of decadence which
infused Symbolist poetry. The most devastating image of the soul is a
mutation of one which we met earlier in a happier context. It is the
metaphor of the soul-boat, which in Shelley aspired toward paradise,
but in Baudelaire was impeded and lost, clumsily burdened with its
freight; finally in Verlaine it is the symbol of shipwreck:

Lasse de vivre, ayant peur de mourir, pareille
Au brick perdu jouet de flux et de reflux,
Mon âme pour d'affreux naufrages appareille.[20]

Weary of living and fearful of dying, like a lost brig, a pawn of the
flux and reflux, my soul prepares for frightful shipwrecks.

Although I spoke about Verlaine earlier, I have kept this image to the
end because it is dramatically in tune with the nihilistic tone with
which Mallarmé, though rarely using the word 'soul', sets the pitch of
annihilation of the soul. Verlaine's 'soul', as an object of flux and
reflux, is totally controlled by outside forces and is a pawn of materialistic determinism. Mallarmé, sparse in his use of the word, echoes
Verlaine with a curt but succinct expression: 'mon âme vide'.[21]

As we approach the end of the century we note that the drama of
the soul's vacillation and alternating ascent and descent disappears.
There is no longer contrast and struggle. We are faced with a static
landscape as opposed to a vertiginous journey. Far from the heights and
depths of the ocean, the soul is set in old solitary parks, motionless,
stolid and pale. There is no longer striving. There is no longer depth.

As it were, the soul surfaces to the level of appearance and is burdened with the monotony of physical reality. The only image left is that of the dead soul, which will be the central metaphor of the following chapter.

6   The Post-Symbolists: the Winter of the Soul

At the turn of the century, Yeats' essay 'The Autumn of the Body' (1898) offers tangible clues to the final waning of the soul. In general, the poet-critic assesses the decadence rampant in both English and Continental poetic writings. Indeed, we have seen that the Symbolists moved steadily toward the stylization of dead soul imagery; so in English minor Decadent poets such as J. A. Symonds, Francis Thompson, Lord Alfred Douglas, and Richard Le Gallienne there was a parallel pattern. In the poem 'The Decadent to his Soul' (1892) Le Gallienne does not concern himself with investing the soul with the accoutrements of imagery. He perceives it as a separate entity, and describes it as a separate being whom he confronts in dialogue:

> The Decadent was speaking to his soul;
> Poor useless thing, he said,
> Why did God burden me with such as thou?
> The body were enough,
> The body gives me all.[1]

Ironically, it is not the body that burdens the soul, but rather the soul that burdens the body. The mingling of the two components is suggested by the reference to an incestuous relationship:

> He dreamed of a new sin:
> An incest 'twixt the body and the soul.[2]

A 'hollow hectic face' suggests the soul's barrenness and is indeed its most distinct quality. This poem of Le Gallienne's is one among many written by his contemporaries in this period. Many of them employ this same dialectic form of contempt and challenge.

But Yeats observes that the decadence afflicting spirituality, omnipresent in the period, is not merely a passing phenomenon of spleen; rather it is a profound ailment attacking and jeopardizing the soul's survival. Of the various examples offered to the poet of this devastating mood before him, the poet Maeterlinck supplies Yeats with the increasingly characteristic dead state of the soul. In particular, Yeats notices the visible change in the theatre in contrasting a dramatist such as Villiers de l'Isle Adam with Maeterlinck. Villiers de l'Isle Adam does not seem to capture the total collapse of the soul as his follower Maeterlinck does:

> ... Count Villiers de l'Isle Adam swept together, by what seemed a sudden energy, words behind which glimmered a spiritual and passionate mood, as the flame glimmers behind the dusky blue and red glass in an Eastern lamp; and created persons from whom has fallen all even of personal characteristic except a thirst for that hour when all things shall pass away like a cloud, and pride like that of the Magi following their star over many mountains; while Maeterlinck has plucked away even this thirst and this pride and set before us *faint souls*, naked and pathetic shadows already half vapour and sighing to one another upon the border of the last abyss.[3]

Whereas Yeats qualifies the physical manifestation of this decline as the 'autumn of the body', he does not have a label for the annihilation of the soul.

It is through reference to the weariness of the body that Yeats implies the condition of the soul. He observes that the artist at the end of the century was expressing a reality which had been gradually divested of the illusions of spiritual substance:

> Man has wooed and won the world, and has fallen weary, and not I think, for a time, but with a weariness that will not end until the last autumn, when the stars shall be blown away like withered leaves. He grew weary when he said, 'These things that I touch are alone real,' for he saw them without illusion at last, and found them but air and dust and moisture.[4]

As the poet considers reality in terms of its inherent mortality, we detect in our identification of soul imagery the same process occurring whereby this immanent sense of mortality invades the dominion of the soul itself, terminating the autumn of the body with the winter of the soul.

The collection of poems most pertinent in terms of crystallizing metonymies of the soul at the turn of the century is Stefan George's *Das Jahr der Seele* (1897). Here it is not a question of detecting the actual use of the word since the entire set of poems alludes to the various movements and designations of the soul. The sense of the soul is derived from contexts evoking unfulfilled love, lack of communication, sterile human relationships, abuse of sensitivity and a general pervasive mood of emptiness pervading the earthly scene. Reconciled as the speaker and his addressee are to the emptiness of their metaphysical state, they engage in a mock drama of life, gesturing to each other in a cold, dispassionate manner. Having no illusion, they fail to suffer the consequences of disillusion. The sequence of poems captures the soul in various phases of its decline and inactivity.

Many commentators have noted the exclusion of the season of spring in the tracing of the passage of the soul through the metaphoric states of autumn (*Nach der Lese*), winter (*Waller im Schnee*) and summer (*Sieg des Sommers*). Indeed, in contrast to the poetic notion of the soul's year in Hölderlin from which George's title is derived, spring and its metaphoric significance is distinctly absent.

Rather than spring, the winter of the soul is its most valid characterization and becomes its metonymy. The key poem central to the unravelling of the significance of the soul is 'Wo die strahlen schnell verschleissen' which concludes the section *Waller im Schnee*:

Wo die strahlen schnell verschleissen
Leichentuch der kahlen auen
Wasser sich in furchen stauen
In den sümpfen schmelzend gleissen.

Und zum strom vereinigt laufen:
Türm ich für erinnerungen
Spröder freuden die zerspringen
Une für dich den scheiterhaufen.

Weg den schritt vom brande lenkend
Greif ich in dem boot die ruder-
Drüben an dem strand ein bruder
Winkt das frohe banner schwenkend.

Tauwind fährt in ungestümen
Stössen über brache schollen.
Mit den welken seelen sollen
Sich die pfade neu beblümen. (p. 33)[5]

When the shining rays swiftly strike a shroud of bare pastures, water in the furrows does stand and in the flashing softened swamps does shine. And by the dashing united rivers, I evoke for memories brittle joys which are cracking, and for you the funeral pyres. My step guided away from the blaze, I grasp the oars in the boat – yonder on the shore a brother waving the blithe banner, flags. The dewy thawing wind travels in tumult, thrusting itself over fallow lands. With the withered soul shall the paths be reflowered.

The 'withered souls' or 'welken seelen' are intrinsic to the general image of the wasteland which is the principle landscape of the poem. The soul is in contact with those aspects which represent barrenness of the human condition as made manifest in the images relating to emptiness, frost and stagnation. For example, in the first stanza there is reference to the bare pastures ('die kahlen auen') and to stagnant swamps ('Wasser sich in furchen stauen/In den sümpfen schmelzend gleissen'). Ironically, the attempt at thawing the ice and removing the barrier of frost is undermined by the condition at the end of the poem which describes the perpetual reflowing of the plains with souls of a withered condition.

Interpreted as an ironic love poem, even the memories which are described as brittle ('sproder freuden') are effaced as the soul attempts a withdrawal from the scene of love. The reference to the winking brother in the third stanza suggests the universality of the soul's state. The refurbishing of the plain with new withered souls points to the endless cycle of dying souls. The thawing of the snow does not provide an accompanying revival and blossoming of soul.

Of the climates used as correlatives of the soul's condition, winter then is most characteristic. The souls are most often withering on waste plains of discontent. The opening poem of 'Nach der Lese' in fact points to the ironic gathering of the dead and decaying flowers before the advent of frost which represents its ultimate condition. In the place of outright reference to states of soul through specific uses of the word, the landscapes both of the wasteland or more especially of the familiar dead park ('der totgesagte Park') opening the collection are the trigger for the soul's designation. In fact, in the opening poem, the poet invites the reader to witness the dying of the soul as he beckons him into the dead park to gather the dead and fading souls:

'Komm in den totgesagten Park und schau . . .'

Elsewhere, as in the poem 'In freien viereck mit den gelben steinen', additional aspects of the soul's condition are conveyed in the further characterization of the park scene which includes empty stone, fountains, and dead birch branches. The scene is still and silent under the shadow of the moon:

Im freien viereck mit den gelben steinen
In dessen mitte sich die brunnen regen
Willst du noch flüchtig späte rede pflegen
Da heut dir hell wie nie die sterne scheinen.

Doch tritt von dem basaltenen behälter!
Er winkt die toten zweige zu bestatten
Im vollen mondenlichte weht as kälter
Als drüben unter jener föhren schatten.

Ich lasse meine grosse traurigkeit
Dich falsch erraten um dich zu verschonen
Ich fühle hat die zeit uns kaum entzweit
So wirst du meinen traum nicht mehr bewohnen

Doch wenn erst unterm schnee der park entschlief
So glaub ich das noch leiser trost entquille
Aus manchen schönen resten – strauss und brief –
In tiefer Kalter winterlicher stille. (p. 22)

In the open square with the yellow stones in whose centre the fountain waters spring, though late in the day you will still nurse your
discourse, since to you the stars never shone so brightly. But tread
away from the basalt basin! It signals to bury the dead branches. In
full moonlight it blows colder than yonder, under those pine-tree
shades. I have let you misconstrue my great sorrow so as to spare you;
methinks once time has hardly divided us, you will no longer inhabit
my dream. Yet when first the park slumbers under snow, then, I
believe, slight comforts may spring forth from many lovely remains –
bloom and note – in the deep frigid winter stillness.

Thematically, the poem deals with unfulfilled love in which the souls
cloistered in the dead park[6] engaged in meaningless parley. At the
centre of the park is the basalt cavity which is the receptacle of the
dead souls when talking ceases and mere vestiges of past intercourse
remain as fragments or shadows. The aura of silence reigns, suggested
by the frigid winter stillness: 'in tiefer kalter winterlicher stille.'

Finally, aside from the key images of wasteland, dead parks and
withering flowers which closely mirror the soul's state, there is a particular gesture which graphically conveys the soul and its emptiness.
Empty hands raised into empty spaces and blank eyes peering out from
blank faces appear in the poem 'Die blume die ich mir am fenster hege':

Nun heb ich wieder meine leeren augen
Und in die leere nacht die leeren hände. (p. 31)

Now again do I raise my empty eyes and into the empty night my
empty hands.

This peculiar expression correlates the state of soul, and the foreboding
German adjective 'leer', the equivalent of the French 'néant' is used as
the principal qualifier. The mood results from having severed all rela-
tions with life, symbolized in the cutting of the stem of the already
fading and ailing flower. Devoid of spiritual essence, the physical is all
that remains, and its constituents in terms of eyes and hands spell its
empty substance.

The characterization of dead souls in dry months is not peculiar to
George. It is strikingly present in other major poets of the time in the
passage from the nineteenth to the twentieth century: Hofmannsthal,
Rilke and T. S. Eliot.

Hofmannsthal's 'Psyche' (1892) offers us an example of the dead
state of the soul expressed as a persona rather than through the use of
metaphor or patterns of imagery. The poem is a dialogue between self
and soul in which the soul rejects both life and dream as dead states.
The condition of the soul throughout the conversational poem is that
of dying. The poem is a portrait of a soul weary unto death. So speaks
the wearied soul:

Herr, ich möchte sterben.
Ich bin zum Sterben müde und mich friert. (p. 69)[7]

Sir, I would like to die. I am weary and am freezing unto death.

The words form an echoing refrain aggravating the ailment of the soul. The attempt on the part of the self to promote either life or dream is rejected by the soul which perceives only a dead life before her:

Das Leben hat
Nicht Glanz und Duft. Ich bin es müde, Herr. (p. 70)

Life has not sparkle nor fragrance. I am weary of it, Sir.

Though the poem 'Psyche' contains no outright metaphor of the soul, the meaning of the soul best relates to the traditional soul image of the butterfly, here suggested rather than designated. But the butterfly, which is generally a symbol of metamorphosis, here fails to achieve that final state of eternal existence. Rather it is in perpetual motion best described in terms of the movement of fluttering which translates the restless and anxious quality of its mortal existence. In examples drawn from Hofmannsthal's lyrics, specific key words and general landscapes are operative in substantiating this characterization of the soul.

The poem 'Lebenslied' (1896) conveys the uncertain quality of the soul and the movements of fluttering and fluctuation which are indigenous to it. We notice the key image of the soul carried along in a throng of bees:

Der Schwarm von wilden Bienen
Nimmt seine Seele mit; (p. 12)

The swarm of wild bees takes his soul along with them.

In fact the notion of the bees and its associations are multiplied into images of singing dolphins and flowing rivers:

Das Singen von Delphinen
Beflügelt seinen Schritt:
Ihn tragen alle Erden
Mit mächtigen Gebärden.
Der Flüsse Dunkelwerden
Begrenzt den Hirtentag!

The singing of the dolphins quickens his step: all earth supports him with mighty gestures. The darkening of the rivers binds the herdsman's day.

The soul surrenders to the forces of physical existence and in so doing adopts its motions all leading eventually to death. The entire life landscape which the poem paints relates specifically to the soul's movements.

The movement which the soul adopts is foreboding. Pervasive is the suggestion of souls carried along a river which is darkening: 'der Flüsse Dunkelwerden.' It relates to the reference of the gliding of the dead in the first stanza of the poem:

> Die Toten, die entgleiten
> Die Wipfel in dem Weiten. (p. 13)

The dead that glide away; treetops in the distance.

The password to the movement of the soul is *Tod*: death underlies the various manifestations of currents and movements.

In a sonnet devoted to the soul 'Sonnet der Seele' (1891) we notice references to rotting and to chains:

> Wenn wir unsrer Seele lauschen,
> Hören wir wie Eisen klirren
> Rätselhafte Quellen rauschen. (p. 496)

When we listen to our souls, it is as if we hear iron clanking and enigmatic springs rushing.

The soul appears a trapped and captured animal in a world enslaved. Interestingly, the reference to the flight of birds does not receive the usual connotation of transcendence:

> Stille Vögelflüge schwirren . . .

Hushed flights of birds whirring . . .

There is a general sense of surrender to the forces of the outer word.

One of the principal words used to designate the soul is 'erschrocken' of shock before blankness and void. In 'Manche freilich . . .' (1895) 'erschrocken' qualifies the soul in its reaction to dumbness:

> Noch weghalten von der erschrockenen Seele
> Stummes Niederfallen ferner Sterne (p. 19)

Yet keep from the startled soul the silent falling of distant stars

The soul contacts dumbness and is startled in its presence. The word 'stumm' or silence is obsessively related to the muting and deadening forces which persistently confront the soul and annul the power of the inner world. The portrait is that of a soul struck and paralysed by the death experience. In contrast to the same paralysing effect which was temporary in Hölderlin's pattern of the soul, here it has a finality. The soul cannot dismiss ('abtun') or keep away ('weghalten') the dumbness which is germane to *Dasein* or existence.

Personification of a dead soul is also to be found in Rilke's poem 'Orpheus, Eurydike, Hermes' from the *Neue Gedichte* (1907–8). The poem contains a reservoir of dead soul imagery: there is both the individual dead soul of Eurydike and the general subterranean earth-scape which harbours her. The word 'soul' used in the first line of the poem is replaced by both a series of images which follow and charac-terizations rather than by single, separate metaphors. Here is an in-stance in which the entire poem becomes a metonymy of the soul:

> Das war der Seelen wunderliches Bergwerk,
> Wie stille Silbererze gingen sie
> als Adern durch sein Dunkel. Zwischen Wurzeln
> entsprang das Blut, das fortgeht zu den Menschen
> und schwer wie Porphyr sah es aus wie im Dunkel.
> Sonst war nichts Rotes.
>
> Felsen waren da
> und wesenlose Wälder. Brücken über Leeres
> und jener grosse graue blinde Teich,
> der über seinem fernen Grunde hing
> wie Regenhimmel über einer Landschaft.
> Und zwischen Wiesen, sanft und voller Langmut,
> erschien des einen Weges blasser Streifen,
> wie eine lange Bleiche hingelegt. (p. 542)[8]

That was the strange mine of souls. Like silent silver ore they mark a sinuous path of veins through its darkness. Between roots spirts the blood that goes forth to men, and with the intensity of porphyry it glowed in the darkness. No other red was there. And there were rocks and shadowy forests. Brooks over emptiness and that big grey blind pond that hung over its distant bottom like a rainy sky over a landscape. And between meadows, soft and full of patience, there appeared a pale streak of a pathway lying like a long bleached track.

An examination of the earthscape designated in the above passage supplies us with imagery relating to the dead state of the soul. We ob-serve its constituency composed of roots, hard rocks, stones, shadowy forests, empty regions, and grey stagnant ponds. A general atmosphere of a bleached expanse is strikingly apparent in the designation and relates to the emptiness characteristic of the scene of the soul.

The scene is thereby laid for the passage of the dead souls along the labyrinthine passageways of the underworld. The dead souls are twisted and twined, nurtured in rock, not in fertility.

Muteness is omnipresent. There is significance in the fact that Or-pheus, wandering through the underworld loses the use of his lyre and is thus mute:

Voran der schlanke Mann im blauen Mantel
der stumm und ungeduldig vor sich aussah.
Ohne zu kauen frass sein Schritt den Weg
in grossen Bissen; seine Hände hingen
schwer und verschlossen aus dem Fall der Falten
und wussten nicht mehr von der leichten Leier,
die in die Linke eingewachsen war
wie Rosenranken in den Ast des Olbaums. (p. 543)

At the head the slender man in the blue mantle, dumb and impatient, looked out before him. Without chewing, his step devoured the road in large bites; his hands hung heavily and were closed and clasped and knew no longer of the gentle lyre which had grown into his left like twining roses in a branch of olive.

His hands are heavy and cannot produce music. Steadily the emphasis is upon the lack of communication between him and Eurydike.

The figure of Eurydike is the dead soul incarnate. Like the figure of Samain's Infanta, she is marked by characteristics which point to her sterility. The soul is sexless, untouchable, virginal, closed as an evening flower:

Sie war in einem neuen Mädchentum
und unberührbar; ihr Geschlecht war zu
wie eine junge Blume gegen Abend. (p. 544)

She was in a new virginity and untouchable; her sex did close as a young flower does towards evening.

Impotency is conveyed in terms of the hands which are withdrawn, says the poet, from the communion offered in marriage. They are pale and closed. They do not reach out toward *the other*:

und ihre Hände waren der Vermählung
so sehr entwöhnt, dass selbst des leichten Gottes
unendlich leise, leitende Berührung
sie kränkte wie zu sehr Vertraulichkeit. (pp. 544–5)

And her hands were so very much removed from the bonds of marriage that even the infinitely light touch of the god leading her offended her as being too great an intimacy.

So alien is the soul from intimacy of any nature that the contact with the god, Hermes, anguishes her.

In particular, the hardening and calculation of the soul is suggested through the characterization of Eurydike's bond with rock and roots:

Sie war schon aufgelöst wie langes Haar
und hingegeben wie gefallner Regen
und ausgeteilt wie hundertfacher Vorrat.

Sie war schon Wurzel. (p. 545)

She was already loosened like long hair and given forth like fallen rain and dealt out like a manifold of goods. She was already rooted.

Whereas in Hölderlin we have observed how Hyperion went in search of the dead Diotima and found response of love across the centuries of separation, here where according to the legend the separation has only been a short one we detect a total break as if an amputation of the soul from the body has occurred. The inter-soul communication has been silenced.

Decidedly, the soul as presented by Rilke lacks the power of love, demonstrated most powerfully in Eurydike's relationship with Orpheus. She fails to respond to the beckoning of Orpheus. Trapped in herself, she is cloistered:

Sie war in sich, wie Eine hoher Hoffnung,
und dachte nicht des Mannes, der voranging,
und nicht des Weges, der ins Leben aufstieg.
Sie war in sich. Und ihr Gestorbensein
erfüllte sie wie Fülle. (p. 544)

She was withdrawn into herself like one with a high hope, and thought not of the man who went before them, nor of the road which ascended into life. She was withdrawn into herself. And her dead being filled her as fullness.

Ironically, her only fullness is in terms of death, which bars the entry of life. She fails to comprehend Orpheus or even to recognize him. When the messenger Hermes tells her of him, she is oblivious and responds as if in total ignorance of his identity:

Er hat sich umgewendet –
begriff sie nichts und sagte leise: Wer? (p. 545)

He has turned round – She understood nothing and softly uttered: Who?

The final episode offers a dramatic correlative of the empty soul: Orpheus glances at the figure of Eurydike only to note that she leaves with Hermes, unprepared to leave the domain of death and enter contact with life.

In fine, the deteriorization of the Orpheus myth is relevant to the final states of the evolution of the soul. Contrary to the standard interpretation of the myth where it is Orpheus' fault that Eurydike cannot join him again, here it is Eurydike's fault since the soul has now been conceived as a human principle, mortal as life itself, rather than one of eternal existence fortified by the passage into death.

The foregoing observations enable us to understand a particular facet of Eliot which is in the context of this slow but steady involution we have traced in the aspiration toward immortality. Although in the later and perhaps better known part of his poetic career, Eliot submits to conversion and reinforced Christian faith, there is a point in his development when he takes part in the general attitude of decadence and subsists in the degeneration of that element of the immortal which is the soul.

He presents us with a set of correlatives for the soul's dead state. This is particularly lucid in *Preludes* (1915), in which the soul is situated in a context of sterile love, boredom and void. The four sections which constitute the poem's sequence set the soul in frames of urban environments. The soul is viewed from various angles of vision, all pointing to its vacancy, as in the case of Rilke. The landscape portraits of the soul provide an objectification of the spiritual void.

The constitution of the soul has changed. Take, for example, the reference to the soul's sordidity in the description of the woman:

> You dozed, and watched the night revealing
> The thousand sordid images
> Of which your soul was constituted;
> They flickered against the ceiling.
> And when all the world came back
> And the light crept up between the shutters
> And you heard the sparrows in the gutters,
> You had such a vision of the street
> As the street hardly understands;
> Sitting along the bed's edge, where
> You curled the papers from your hair,
> Or clasped the yellow soles of feet
> In the palms of both soiled hands. (p. 23)[9]

The dreary images of which the soul is constituted are delineated in terms of the urban scene containing gutters and pavement or in terms of the correlatives suggesting the least spiritual parts of the human body: soiled hand and soles of feet. There is in fact a pun on the word 'soul' which succeeds in reducing it to the sordidness of feet: 'yellow soles'. Qualified by the adjective 'yellow', the soul is associated with other major correlatives of fog and smoke.

Indeed, the soul acquires the heaviness of a ceiling of fog and the acerbity of a city pavement;

> His soul stretched tight across the skies
> That fade behind a city block,
> Or trampled by insistent feet
> At four and five and six o'clock.

Steadily it receives the connotation of a physical presence which is wrought and abused: it is 'stretched' and 'trampled'.

The season identified with the soul is again winter as the opening lines make readily apparent:

> The winter evening settles down
> With smells of steaks in passageways. (p. 22)

Emptiness of the soul is also suggested in the frequent reference to the 'vacant lots'.

There is an overt sense of the soul's fragmentation revealed through the various images interspersed suggestive of scraps, pieces, and remains;

> The burnt-out ends of smoky days.
> And now a gusty shower wraps
> The grimy scraps
> Of withered leaves about your feet. (p. 22)

Further images suggesting the materiality of the soul are to be found in 'Morning at the Window' (1917):

> They are rattling breakfast plates in basement kitchens,
> And along the trampled edges of the street
> I am aware of the damp souls of housemaids
> Sprouting despondently at area gates.
>
> The brown waves of fog toss up to me
> Twisted faces from the bottom of the street,
> And tear from a passer-by with muddy skirts
> An aimless smile that hovers in the air
> And vanishes along the level of the roofs. (p. 27)

The physical term 'dampness' is attributed to the soul, endowing it with a languid character. The soul is no longer the seat of aesthetic values, rather it assumes the character of ugliness, made visual in the reference to the deformed and 'twisted faces'.

Neither is the soul free. It is enslaved as the reference to the housemaids in the above passage suggests. Whereas we have witnessed the soul's soaring in earlier poets, here we identify souls that are incarcerated. It is to be noted that the adjective 'aimless' refers to the soul's floundering and the lack of will or self-direction.

But where the preceding instances succeed in conveying the sterility of the soul through a vast array of imagery and settings, a poem such as 'Whispers of Immortality' (1920) provides us with a statement concerning its dissipation. In a poem on immortality one would expect the extolling of the soul. Instead, we have a keen sense of its absence.

We are drawn to observe how man makes the absence of the soul concrete. Highly suggestive is the reference to the marrow:

> He knew the anguish of the marrow
> The ague of the skeleton;
> No contact possible to flesh
> Allayed the fever of the bone. (p. 52)

In negative terms, Eliot depicts the soul as cold and dead: there is a vain effort to keep it warm:

> And even the Abstract Entities
> Circumambulate her charm;
> But our lot crawls between dry ribs
> To keep our metaphysics warm. (p. 53)

We realize that originally what was abstract had become living and concrete. Suddenly by placing the soul on another level of abstraction Eliot forcefully conveys its evaporation.

Finally, in 'Animula' (1929) Eliot traces the struggle of the soul and brings it to its agony. It is astounding to see to what extent unconsciously this aspect of the soul has entered his thinking; that even after he is converted he can speak of the soul in such terms:

> The heavy burden of the growing soul
> Perplexes and offends more, day by day . . .
> The pain of living and drug of dreams
> Curl up the small soul in the window seat
> Behind the Encyclopaedia Britannica.
> Issues from the hand of time the simple soul
> Irresolute and selfish, misshapen, lame,
> Unable to fare forward or retreat,
> Fearing the warm reality, the offered good,
> Denying the importunity of the blood. (p. 107)

Though the word 'soul' is used, the descriptions relate more specifically to the body. Visibly we witness its waning as it assumes the deteriorating character of old age. Accretion and erosion of the soul are conveyed. There is also a strong sense of its paralysis:

> Unable to fare forward or retreat

as well as its frigidity:

> Denying the importunity of the blood.

Its most telling attribute is its debility expressed in human terms of lameness, fear, irresolution and withdrawal. There are images relating to its reduction, as in the reference to the shadows and scepters;

Shadow of its own shadows, sceptre in its own gloom. (p. 107)

Where in Wordsworth the soul preserves its link with childhood, in Eliot the soul yields to the mortal process of deterioration and identifies itself with old age.

Even after the agony the soul is dead with all the ceremonies attending the Christian death of the body:

Living first in the silence after the viaticum. (p. 107)

Of course, there is controversy over the interpretation of the viaticum and the conclusions at which T. S. Eliot arrives. While some are convinced that Eliot leads the soul to eventual resurrection in the after-life (making this a joyous poem), others believe that it is in fact the epitome of earthly resignation.[10]

We are not obliged to be an arbitrator in this dispute since the focus here is not interpretation but elucidation of the metaphoric changes and evolutions that project the soul concept. The association of the soul with the very terminology of the last rites provides us indeed with the most total identification of soul and body that we have yet perceived.

Inevitably the associations of Eliot's poem with one of the first instances of the soul concept that we have examined is not to be overlooked. Haunting is Wordsworth in the title 'Whispers of Immortality' and in the lines of 'Animula'. Eliot appears to counter Wordsworth's earlier poetic statement on the soul's immortality and the celestial apparel with which the typical Romantic poet clothed the soul. Where there were intimations of immortality in the earlier poet and in the climate which he reflected, here the intimations have become whispers, which like the correlatives of the withered leaves, fade and disappear.

7   The Stylistic Alchemy

The significant images of the soul running through Western nineteenth-century poetry have thus far been sought out; the progression in form and function of these poetic references brings to light several kinds of change; the recognition of these can provide a basis of synthesis. As Todorov says:

> Isoler un élément au cours de l'analyse n'est qu'un procédé de travail; sa signification se trouve dans ses rapports avec les autres.[1]

> To isolate an element in the course of an analysis is only an operation; its signification lies in its relation with others.

But before trying to record these transformations according to the shiftings of linguistic signifiers, a closer look at Wordsworth becomes necessary. Observations in his work of the location of the soul, form of address to the soul, and the destination of the soul are the standard Romantic determinants which are later affected. After this initial scrutiny, these transformations will be classified in terms of substitutions, changing vital processes, and finally a fundamental rhetorical alteration that is a symptom of the total disruption of the concept.

The obvious point of departure then is the 'Intimations' ode, where as we know the word 'soul' occupies a central position. Implied in the very title itself, the specific word 'soul' is diffused into the abstract notion of immortality. It is to be noted that the poem is directed specially at the expostulation of the abstract notion.

The poem proceeds structurally by way of contrast, locating the soul in time and space. Two states are juxtaposed: the *past* in which the soul reigned (the poet's own childhood) and the *present* (the poet recollecting the state of childhood). Analogously, nature, the corresponding world, receives two characterizations: the *past* state in which it was clothed in 'celestial light' (introduced by the adverbial clause 'there was a time') and the *present* state of jubilee (introduced by the adverb 'now').

Two sets of qualifiers reinforce this division. In particular, the words 'glory' and 'splendour' relate to the primal state of soul:

There was a time when meadow, grove, and stream,
The earth, and every common sight,
    To me did seem
Apparelled in celestial light,
The *glory** and the freshness of a dream.
              [stanza I]

Where is it now, the *glory* and the dream?
              [stanza IV]

Forget the *glories* he hath known . . .
              [stanza VI]

Though nothing can bring back the hour
Of *splendour* in the grass, of *glory* in the flower.
              [stanza X]

Aesthetic adjectives of secondary degree such as 'lovely' and 'gay'
relate to the present state:

The Rainbow comes and goes,
And *lovely* is the Rose.
              [stanza II]

And all the earth is *gay*
    Land and sea
Give themselves up to jollity
              [stanza III]

The division sets the soul in the timeless realm of the *past* 'glory' as
opposed to the mortal realm of the *present* festivity.

The soul acquires connotations not only in terms of the contrast
between the past and the present, but also through the dichotomy of
interiority and exteriority. Two states of existence are presented: the
inward world of permanency in which the soul is situated, the *outward*
world of transiency in which the senses are operative. The contrast is
found in the eighth stanza in which the poet addresses the child:

Thou, whose exterior semblance doth belie
    Thy Soul's immensity.

There is also the contrast between the outer vision and the inner vision
of the soul's eye:

Thou best Philosopher, who yet does keep
Thy heritage, thou Eye among the blind.

Overwhelmingly, the soul is identified with light, qualified in the Ode
as the 'celestial light' (stanza II), the 'visionary gleam' (stanza IV), the
'fountain-light' (stanza IX) and the 'master-light' (stanza IX). Aside

* All italics in the illustrative texts of this chapter and the next are mine.

from these abstract expressions, there are metaphors which relate the soul specifically to *day*:

> Thou, over whom thy Immortality,
> Broods like the *Day*;
>   [stanza VIII]

and to the process of *vision*:

> Our Souls have *sight* of that immortal sea ...
>   [stanza IX]

It has already been observed that the fundamental state to which the soul relates is childhood. Language denoting the child, then is concurrently descriptive of the soul. The child receives hyperbolic dimensions as the container of the prodigious soul:

> Thou, whose exterior semblance doth belie
>   Thy Soul's *immensity* ...
>   Mighty Prophet! Seer blest! ...
> Thou little Child, yet glorious in the *might* ...
>   [stanza VIII]

The child is addressed by the poet with the deferential pronoun 'thou'. Elsewhere, in *The Prelude*, the state of childhood is personified in a declarative statement:

> Our simple childhood, sits upon a throne. (v, 508)

Aside from the descriptive factors relating to the glory of the past, the light, and the child, which are frames for the soul, there are a series of relationships which also serve to qualify the soul. The soul is evoked in terms of the master in the master-slave relationship:

> Thou, over whom thy Immortality
>   Broods like the Day, a *Master* o'er a *Slave*.
>   [stanza VIII]

The soul relates to the palace in the palace-prison relationship:

> And that imperial *palace* whence he [the child] came ...
>   [stanza VI]

> Shades of the *prison*-house begin to close
>   Upon the growing Boy.
>   [stanza V]

The soul relates to the liberty in the liberty-tyrrany relationship:

> Delight and *liberty*, the simple creed
> Of Childhood ...
>   [stanza IX]

Why with such earnest pains dost thou provoke
The years to bring the inevitable *yoke*.

[stanza VIII]

In the three instances the soul dominates.

Here, then, are the basic contexts in which the soul is set in the 'Intimations' ode. Additional examples drawn from *The Prelude* substantiate the above mentioned qualities. A derivative of the child image is to be found in the image of the elfin pinnace of the first book of *The Prelude*:

A little *boat* tied to a willow tree
Within a rocky cave, its usual home.
Straight I unloosed her *chain*, and stepping in,
Pushed from the shore ...

She was an *elfin pinnace*; lustily
I dipped my oars into the silent lake,
And, as I rose upon the stroke, my *boat*
Went heaving through the water like a *swan*;
When, from behind that craggy steep till then
The horizon's bound, a huge peak, black and huge,
As if with voluntary power instinct
Upreared its head. (I, 358–61; 373–80)

There are a cluster of references to the childhood state, particularly suggested by the word 'elfin' and by the action of the unloosening of the chain. The incident highlights the sight as the primary characteristic of the soul. Interestingly, in retrospect it can be stated that the pinnace and the swan are substitutes of the soul. Here are the ingredients for two fundamental metaphors of boat and bird which relate to the soul and here unconsciously find their origin in a natural scene. These will be seen as prevailing in the future lyricism relating to the soul.

The episode of the ascent of Mount Snowdon in the last book of *The Prelude* associates the heights of elevation with the soul:

For instantly a light upon the turf
Fell like a flash, and lo! as I looked up,
The moon hung naked in a firmament
Of *azure without cloud*, and at my feet
Rested a silent sea of hoary mist ...
Not so the *ethereal vault*; encroachment none
Was there, nor loss; only the inferior stars
Had disappeared, or shed a fainter light
In the *clear presence* of the full-orbed Moon.
Who, from her *sovereign elevation*, gazed

Upon the billowy ocean, as it lay
All meek and silent. (xiv, 38–42, 50–6)

The poet proceeds to consider the vision as an emblem of the mind, but
the characteristics which are offered relate more specifically to the soul:

There I beheld the emblem of a mind
That feeds upon infinity, that *broods*
Over the dark abyss . . .
         . . . A mind sustained
By recognitions of *transcendent* power,
In sense conducting to ideal form,
In soul of more than mortal privilege.
One function, above all, of such a mind
Had Nature shadowed there, by putting forth,
'Mid circumstances awful and *sublime*,
That mutual *domination* which she loves
To exert upon the face of outward things,
So moulded, joined, abstracted, so endowed,
With interchangeable *supremacy*. (xiv, 70–3; 75–84)

In the first passage cited there is a cluster of references to sky images,
including the clear azure and the ethereal vault. The image of the
moon and its supreme point of elevation is highlighted. In the second
passage the mind is elevated as it broods over the dark abyss. It is to
be noted that in the 'Intimations' ode, 'brood' is a verb used with
immortality (line 119). This particular verb is functional in denoting
the looming and elevation of the soul, and is the common denominator
to soul and mind in Wordsworth: it links the passage of *The Prelude*
relating to the mind with that of the Ode relating to soul.

Aside from the concrete images relating to elevation of soul, there
are abstract words in the second passage cited above, such as 'transcendent', 'sublime', 'domination' and 'supremacy', which denote the
imperial power of the soul. The kingly, stately aspect of its presence is
emphasized by the 'privilege' which relates to the soul and to its dominant position in the two relationships of master-slave and palace-prison
mentioned earlier. Both in the Ode and in *The Prelude* the soul is at
the top of the hierarchy.

The above instances are examples in which descriptions of incidents
function as periphrases of the quality of the soul. Besides entire episodes, there are certain phrases, diffused throughout the work, which
are periphrases of the soul. First, there is the word 'presence' which is
suggestive of life:

Ye Presences of Nature in the sky
And on the earth! Ye visions of the hills
And Souls of lonely places (i, 464–6)

There is also the phrase 'sentiment of Being', suggestive of essence:

> I felt the sentiment of Being spread
> O'er all that moves and all that seemeth still (II, 401–2)

The two expressions are combined in the term 'living presence' (V, 34). Particularly characteristic of the soul are elements relating to life and vitality, as in the expression 'vital soul' (I, 150). Another expression related to the soul is 'under-power':

> To lack the first great gift, the vital soul
> Nor general truths, which are themselves a sort
> Of Elements and Agents, *Under-Powers* (I, 150–2)

There are also periphrases regarding its immortality as in 'the immortal spirit':

> Dust as we are, the *immortal spirit* grows
> Like harmony in music; there is a dark
> Inscrutable workmanship that reconciles
> Discordant elements, makes them cling together
> In one society. (I, 340–4)

and in 'immortal being':

> ... to think that our immortal being
> No more shall need such garments ... (V, 23–4)

Finally, 'breath and everlasting motion' and 'the eternity of thought' periphrase the soul:

> Thou Soul that are *the eternity of thought,*
> That givest to forms and images *a breath*
> *And everlasting motion* ... (I, 402–4)

The frequency of the figure of the periphrase is appropriate to the description of the sublime, the most fitting qualification of the soul. In discussing the sublime, Longinus has stated:

> Just as in music what we call ornament enhances the beauty of the main theme, so periphrasis often chimes with the literal expression of our meaning and gives it a far richer note, especially if it is not bombastic or discordant but agreeably in harmony.[2]

It can be concluded that the use of periphrasis by Wordsworth is stylistic evidence of the intangibility ascribed to the soul in the early Romantic context. Imagery, episode, and context were periphrastic. The concreteness of the metaphor was significantly lacking. In the line of poets since early Romanticism, there is an entire spectrum of rhetorical devices, ranging from image to metaphor to metonymy. In this study the fact has emerged that the devices do not progress systematically, but rather are used interchangeably according to the *degree* of objectivity with which the soul is envisaged.

In proceeding to examine the rest of our material we will retain as a gauge the general associations of the soul that have emerged from Wordsworth's periphrastic medium as representative of the early Romantic context. The soul references will be grouped in three sections: specific image, vital process, and rhetorical structure.

I THE IMAGE

The most constant and prevailing of the images is that of the boat. It is true that critics of Romanticism have observed the importance of the journey theme as a symbol of quest in Romantic poetry. For instance R. A. Foakes has referred to this phenomenon in the following manner:

> The figure of a journey is a natural image or impression in which to embody the development of the self-consciousness, the soul, the creative imagination, common themes of the Romantic poets.[3]

But the concern has generally been in the movement of journey rather than in the vehicle and the state of being moved from one place to another. What we have discovered in scrutinizing the journey image in connection with the soul metaphor is that the boat symbol is not merely a displacement symbol but a motive force itself in the act of release and flight. A mortal pinnace in Wordsworth, it undergoes in Shelley rich development, as we have seen. With the emphasis on the movement of the soul in Shelley, the soul-boat's motions are charted:

> My soul is an enchanted boat
> Which, like a sleeping swan, doth float
> Upon the silver waves of thy sweet singing;
> And thine doth like an angel sit
> Beside a helm conducting it,
> Whilst all the winds with melody are ringing . . .
> Meanwhile thy spirit lifts its pinions
> In music's most *serene* dominions;
> Catching the winds that fan that happy heaven.
> And we sail on, away, afar . . .
> Till through Elysian garden islets
> By thee, most beautiful of pilots,
> Where never mortal pinnace glided,
> The boat of my *desire* is guided. (*Prometheus Unbound*)

Where the abstract word 'serene' qualifies the spirit, the more concrete word 'desire' qualifies the soul-boat and brings it into the earthly realm. Where 'spirit' is linked to the element of air and is described by vocabulary relating to the ethereal context, 'soul' is joined to the elements of water ('My soul . . ./Into a sea profound') and earth ('Till through Elysian garden islets . . . The boat of my desire is guided') and described by language relating to the terrestrial context. In general, qualification of the boat is made through the use of nominal forms of compound metaphor rather than through abstract paraphrase. An exhilarated, unreal boat in Shelley, its character and motion have been transformed in Baudelaire:

> Vainement ma raison voulait prendre la barre;
> La tempête en jouant déroutait ses efforts,
> Et mon âme dansait, dansait, vieille gabarre
> Sans mâts, sur une mer monstrueuse et sans bords!
> ('Les Sept Vieillards')

The qualification both of the boat and the sea has undergone mutation: the boat in terms of ageing and debunking, the sea in terms of turbulence. The human dimension is added with the mention of 'barre' (helm) and 'mât' (mast), and attention is drawn to the inadequacy of the man-made boat against the forces of the sea. The repetition of 'dansait' and 'sans mâts' serves to emphasize the futility and disaster. A struggling, real ship in Baudelaire, the boat replaces the word 'soul' in Rimbaud, and undergoes mutation by receiving the qualification of yet another metaphor, the carcass:

> Or moi, bateau perdu sous les cheveux des anses,
> Jeté par l'ouragan dans l'éther sans oiseau,
> Moi dont les Monitors et les voiliers des Hanses
> N'auraient pas repêché le carcasse ivre d'eau. ('Le Bateau Ivre')

The language pointing to the drowning and inebriation invests the soul-boat with a human character: there is the identification of the drowning of the boat with drunkenness. The movement downward is particularly significant. In this instance, the boat qualifies the 'moi' or emerging ego. Submerged in the seas in Rimbaud, it is further reduced to a lost brig in Verlaine:

> Lasse de vivre, ayant peur de mourir, pareille
> Au brick perdu jouet de flux et de reflux,
> Mon âme pour d'affreux naufrages appareille. ('L'Angoisse')

The language continues to stress its passivity. The word 'jouet' (pawn) brings the soul-boat into the context of tragic destiny. The boat is again humanized through the words 'lasse' (weary) and 'appareille' (prepare) and transcends a material character. Prepared for shipwreck in Verlaine, it receives similar treatment in Maeterlinck:

Hélas! mes voeux n'amènent plus
Mon âme aux rives des paupières,
Elle est redescendue au reflux ... ('Aquarium')

A similar movement of sinking is described. The sensual quality of the sea which was sensed in Rimbaud by the mention of the hair is also apparent in Verlaine by the mention of the eyelids ('paupières'): the sea image is joined to the eye image. The thematics of erotic love are suggested by the references to the eyelids ('paupières') and desires ('voeux'). From its shipwrecked condition, the boat is suddenly transformed into an immobile entity in Samain:

Elle est là reflétée aux miroirs d'autrefois
Ainsi qu'une galère oubliée en la rade. (*Au Jardin de L'Infante*)

Qualifiers such as 'oubliée' (forgotten) and 'autrefois' (formerly) point to the boat's uselessness. No movement is traced and a static image is presented of the still boat. The deadly notion suggested here is captured in the movement of the dead in Hofmannsthal which reveals not the boat image, but the boat's newly acquired movement:

Die Toten, die entgleiten ('Lebenslied')

Succinctly, the motion is understood without even the elaboration of metaphor. If Hofmannsthal captures the movement of the boat, George expresses the quality of the transformed waters:

Wasser sich in furchen stauen
In den sümpfen schmelzend gleissen. (*Das Jahr der Seele*)

The verb 'stauen' stresses the standing condition of the boat and the stagnation characteristic of the waters. Finally, the image reaches a culmination in Yeats' *The Shadowy Waters* (1906), which is mentioned here as an apt expression of the final state of the soul rendered through the boat image:

I weep because I've nothing for your eyes
But desolate waters and a battered ship.[4]

Forgael, speaking to Dectora, carries the image to its ultimate form.

In the above instances, attention should be directed to the condition of the ship and to the condition of the waters. The ship becomes in turn elfin, enchanted, old, lost, shipwrecked, standing, drowned, and battered. The waters are successively silvery, monstrous, disordered, deadly, standing, and desolate.

The image of the bird and process of flight are obsessively related to the soul. Prominent first in Hölderlin, the bird receives majestic qualifications in both Hyperion's and Diotima's soul motions:

Diotimas Auge öffnete sich weit: . . . ward lauter Sprache
und Seele, und, als begänne sie den Flug in die Wolken . . .

Dann sucht ich die höchsten Berge mir auf und ihre
Lüfte, and wie ein Adler, dem der blutende Fittich
geheilt ist, regte mein Geist sich im Freien . . . (*Hyperion*)

Then I searched for the highest mountains and their atmosphere,
and like an eagle whose bleeding pinion is healed, my spirit bestirred
in the air.

Although *Geist* rather than *Seele* is used, the two are synonymous in
this context. We have observed the eagle reappear in Shelley, with the
movement of soaring particularly prominent:

My soul spurned the chains of its dismay,
And in the rapid plumes of song
Clothed itself sublime and strong,
(As a young eagle soars the morning clouds among,)
Hovering in verse o'er its accustomed prey. ('Ode to Liberty')

But the struggle of the soul is more apparent in Shelley since the eagle
is set against the image of servitude: the chains. In the symbolism of
Epipsychidion we find that the soul receives, though indirectly, the
characterization of the albatross:

Say, my heart's sister, wilt thou sail with me?
Our bark is an albatross, whose nest
Is a far Eden of the purple East.

Interestingly, we witness a convergence of the two soul images of the
boat and the bird. Where the boat relates to the ideal state of love, the
eagle relates to the ideal state of liberty. We have also seen the bird
image enter the expression of Eichendorff, stressing the destination of
the bird:

Und meine Seele spannte
Weit ihre Flügel aus
Flog durch die stillen Lande
Als flöge sie nach Haus ('Mondnacht')

So too, in Hugo, there is comparable intimacy of the soul-bird and the
heavens:

Mon âme au ciel, son berceau,
Fuira, car dans ta main blanche
Tu tiens ce sauvage oiseau ('Je respire où tu palpites')

From the soaring of the bird, alterations begin to occur as early as
Keats, who tends to undermine the capacity of the bird to soar:

O destiny!
Into a labyrinth now my soul would fly (*Endymion*)

In the case of Baudelaire, the image of the albatross (in the poem of that name, 'L'Albatros', from *Les Fleurs du Mal*) and its associations put him in line with the early Romantics. There is equally, if not more characteristic, however, the image of the bird as the crow:

Mon âme mieux qu'au temps du tiède renouveau
Ouvrira largement ses ailes de corbeau ('Brumes et Pluies')

In fact, here the opening of the wings and the bird image do not imply the traditional flight to the hereafter but rather tie the concept of flight with the earthly condition of fog and heaviness, thereby countering earlier connotations of the soul-bird and the traditional elevation which was suggested. In Mallarmé, a similar but more outright rendition of the transformed significance of the flight is offered in a plain declarative statement of negative flight:

Ce lac dur oublié qu'hante sous le givre
Le transparent glacier des vols qui n'ont pas fui.
('Le Vierge, le Vivace et le Bel Aujourd'hui')

This hard, forgotten lake haunted under the frost by the transparent glacier of flights not flown.

Though the word 'soul' is not used, by this date the association of bird and soul has become firmly established. The final evidence of the alteration of the soul image of the bird is to be found in Hofmannsthal's 'Sonnet der Seele':

Stille Vögelflüge schwirren . . .

Curt and unelaborate, the expression suggests stillness rather than vivacity of flight, circular buzzing ('schwirren') rather than the upward soaring of the early Romantic.

We have observed, then, a negative progression of the bird image from a movement of soaring and an imperial qualification to the inability to fly and a character that is demeaned. As early at Keats, there is a departure from the Romantic image of the soul-bird, which enables us to group Keats with the line of poets proceeding from Baudelaire.

Another constant approximating the soul is the sky. 'An azure without cloud' in Wordsworth, it receives an equal standard of purity in Hölderlin where it is invested with the intangible and abstract quality of ether:

Unsere Seele lebten nun immer freier und schöner zusammen, und alles in und um uns vereinigte sich zu goldenem Frieden . . . und wir und alle Wesen schwebten durch den unendlichen *Äther*. (*Hyperion*)

Our souls now lived ever freer and more beautifully with each other,
and all within and about us united in golden harmony ... and we
and all 'being' were suspended in the infinite ether.

When evoked in the context of the Greeks and their gods it contains the
noble sun god and moon god, and thereby is exalted:

So hast du mein Herz erfreut
Vater Helios! und, wie Endymion,
War ich dein Liebling,
Heilige *Luna* ...
Wie euch meine Seele geliebt! ('Da ich ein Knabe war')

The predominant image of the sun in Hölderlin invades the sky as the
tangible evidence of its clarity and brightness. In Hugo, its clarity and
luminosity is revealed through the reference to the stars and their
sparkling. There, as we have noted, the condition of the sky reflects the
soul's vision though the word *soul* is not used and the 'je' or 'I' is
substituted for it:

J'étais seul près des flots par une nuit d'étoiles
Pas un nuage aux cieux, sur les mers pas de voiles. (*Les Orientales*)

As well as the clarity of the azure, there is, then, the luminosity of night
and in particular, its incandescence. Steadily, however, significant
changes occur in the quality of the sky. The general alteration is the
shift away from the serene and unadulterated quality of its earliest
designation. Already in Shelley, the sky is no longer free of the earth's
qualification:

The soul of man, like unextinguished fire.
Yet burns *toward heaven* with fierce reproach and doubt
                                        (*Prometheus Unbound*)

The implied metaphor of the soul as a volcano and the contact of the
soul with earth serves to link the sky with the terrestrial realm. The
contamination of the sky with the earth is sensed in the language itself,
which in conveying the vacillation of the soul from the depths of earth
to the heights of sky, qualifies the sky as veiled:

A godlike mind soars forth, in its delight
Making earth bare and *veiling* heaven, and when
It sinks, the swarms that dimmed or shared its light
Leave to its kindred lamps the spirit's awful night.(*Adonais*)

Luminous in other instances, it is suddenly veiled in Shelley. Serene in
the early Romantic context, it is dynamic in Shelley.

In the mid-century context a major shift has been detected in the
quality of the sky which is developed steadily through the end of the

century. We first sense the de-purification of the sky in Baudelaire in
the atmosphere of dusk. In 'Crépuscule du Soir' there is the preliminary
description of the sky which serves as an introduction to the soul, evoked
later in the poem:

> Voici le soir charmant, ami du criminel;
> Il vient comme un complice, à pas de loup; le ciel
> *Se ferme* lentement comme une grande alcôve . . .

> Here is the charming evening, friend of the criminal, it comes
> stealthily like an accomplice; the sky closes slowly like a large
> vault.

The verb 'fermer' (close) and the noun 'alcôve' suggest covering,
darkening, enclosure and seclusion. The concrete verb 'fermer' further
suggests the *process* of this phenomenon which affects and afflicts the
sky. The metaphor of the night as an accomplice ('Il vient comme un
complice, à pas de loup') is another concrete rendering of the ominous
darkening of the region of the sky. A similar characterization of the sky
is found in Mallarmé; a misty sky covers the azure:

> Fuyant, les yeux fermés, je le sens qui regarde
> Avec l'intensité d'un remords atterrant,
> Mon âme vide. Où fuir? . . .
> *Brouillards*, montez! Versez vos cendres monotones
> Avec de longs *haillons de brumes dans les cieux*. ('L'Azur')

Here the contrast is even more striking since the poem entitled 'L'Azur'
succeeds in conveying its opposite, a misty sky which is readily identified with the condition of soul. Transformed into mist in Mallarmé, the
image is stylized in Samain's foggy, wintry evening:

> Vague et noyée au fond du *brouillard hiémal*,
> Mon âme est un manoir dont les vitres sont closes.
>
> (*Au Jardin de l'Infante*)

Here the interpenetration of the sky and soul is caught by the stylist,
making the suggestion into an outright identification. The qualification
of the mist as wintry captures an additional deadly, constricting, atmosphere which the sky possesses. We also have seen the instance of Verhaeren's black and soot-laden evening sky:

> Gares de suie et de fumée, où du gaz pleure . . .
> O mon âme du soir, ce Londres noir qui traine en toi! ('Londres')

In T. S. Eliot too, the sky is infiltrated with fog and contaminated by
the dirt and mire of the city:

> His soul stretched tight across the skies (*Preludes*)

It is devastatingly empty in George:

Und in die *leere* Nacht die leeren Hände (*Das Jahr der Seele*)

We have witnessed a transformation of the sky from the intangibility of infinity to the intangibility of nothingness, from the clear azure to the empty space of night. The fogging and veiling have been the metaphoric process by which the mutation of the sky and its associate, the soul, has occurred.

II VITAL PROCESS

If there are significant substitutions for the image itself, there are also transformations in life processes such as ageing, materializing and de-spiritualizing. These changes, too, bear directly upon the mutation of the soul.

The most dramatic transformation is in ageing. In Wordsworth the child and his world were conducive to the soul. Language relating specifically to the child was descriptive of the soul, as previously noted. In Hölderlin the same reciprocal valuation of soul and child is apparent:

Mit den Kindern spielte das hohe Element [substitute for the soul] am schönsten (*Hyperion*)

With children did the high Element play the most beautifully.

In Keats adolescence has replaced childhood as the state linked with soul. The poet writes in his Preface to *Endymion:*

The imagination of a boy is healthy, and the mature imagination of a man is healthy; but *there is a space of life between, in which the soul is in a ferment,* the character undecided, the way of life uncertain, the ambition thick-sighted: thence proceeds mawkishness, and all the thousand bitters which those men I speak of must necessarily taste in going over the following pages.

The word 'fermentation' suggests the transformation in terms of ageing most succinctly. The drastic change occurs in mid-century with Baudelaire's focus on the soul of an old person, particularly evident in the language of the 'Spleen' poem:

L'âme d'un *vieux* poète erre dans la gouttière
Avec la triste voix d'un fantôme frileux ('Spleen: LXXV')

The vocabulary emphasizes the process of the reduction underlying ageing: 'vieux' (in terms of age), 'fantôme' (in terms of shape), 'gouttière' (in terms of the street) and 'error' (in terms of walking); and it qualifies the soul and its container by an aspect of decrepitude. Significantly, old age contaminates the soul-boat in 'Les Sept Vieillards'.

Et mon âme dansait, dansait, *vieille* gabarre

The language of the entire poem relating to old age and its multiplica-
tion in terms of 'spectres', 'lourds tombereaux' (a metaphor of Sisy-
phus-like men), 'vieillards', 'jumeau centenaire', culminates in the
expression of 'vieille gabarre', which can be taken as the equivalent of
'lourds tombereaux' mentioned earlier in the poem. Old age has also
contaminated the flask image of 'Le Flacon':

> Quand on m'aura jeté, vieux flacon désolé,
> Décrepit, poudreux, sale, abject, visqueux, fêle . . .

The reference to Lazarus mentioned earlier, further brings the soul into
the aged context.

In Verlaine, the aged has taken root, as seen in 'Colloque Sentimental':

> Dans le *vieux* parc solitaire et glacé
> Deux formes ont tout à l'heure passé . . .
> Ton coeur bat-il toujours à mon seul nom?
> Toujours vois-tu mon âme en rêve? – Non.

> In the old solitary and frozen park, two forms just now passed by . . .
> Does your heart still beat at my mere name? Do you still see my
> soul in dream? – No.

'Mon âme en rêve' refers to the past state of youth which has been
replaced by old age, intimated through the old park. Finally, we have
noted the most dramatic instance of the ageing process in T. S. Eliot's
'Animula':

> The heavy burden of the *growing* soul . . .
> Issues from the hand of time the simple soul
> Irresolute and selfish, misshapen, *lame*.

Fittingly, the contrast is seen from the juxtaposition of the 'Intimations'
ode with the related 'Animula' at the two poles of our investigation.

A parallel process to ageing is the course from light to heavy in the
qualification of the soul. Here, there is only need to observe the change
in vocabulary. In Wordsworth it has been seen that the soul is antithetical to weight:

> Full soon thy soul shall have her *earthly freight*,
> And custom lie upon thee with a weight,
> Heavy as frost and deep almost as life! ('Intimations' ode)

Other examples drawn from the first half of the century stress the
lightness of soul, as in the description of Diotima:

> . . . stand sanft empor gestreckt die ganze Gestalt, in *leichter*
> Majestat . . . (*Hyperion*)

and in the description of Shelley's 'enchanted boat', where the floating suggests its buoyancy:

It seems to *float* ever, for ever ... (*Prometheus Unbound*)

In the mid-century context of Baudelaire, analogous to the ageing process, the heaviness of the soul appears. Take the instance from 'Les Sept Vieillards':

Je suivais, roidissant mes nerfs comme un héros
Et discutant avec mon âme déjà lasse,
Le faubourg secoué par les *lourds* tombereaux.

Straining my nerves like a hero, and in discourse with my soul already weary, I made my way through the faubourg shaken by heavy carts.

The most vivid example of the heavy soul as it is firmly established is the passage by Richard Le Gallienne:

The Decadent was speaking to his soul;
Poor useless thing, he said,
Why did God *burden* me with such as thou?

('The Decadent to his Soul')

The final instance is that of T. S. Eliot's 'Animula', as a correlative of the process of ageing:

The *heavy* burden of the growing soul.

The shift from light to heaviness corroborates the ageing process and offers the same conclusion.

Language also conveys the de-spiritualizing of the soul. Steadily more sensuous language is used in reference to the soul. The shift is evident in language referring to the five senses and physical substance undergoing alteration.

First, in terms of the five senses, it has been observed that the most spiritual of the five, i.e. sight and hearing were prevalent in the early Romantic context, an emphasis inherited from Swedenborgian idealism. It has been seen that the entire basis of Wordsworth's language denoting the soul is that of vision, perhaps most haunting in the line:

Our Souls have *sight* of that immortal sea ('Intimations' ode)

In Hölderlin the sense of hearing is highlighted in the 'Himmelgesang'. There is the linkage of the soul with heavenly speech:

Diotimas Auge öffnete sich weit ... ward lauter Sprache und Seele
(*Hyperion*)

In Hugo, too, we have noticed the symphony of sound and sight in a passage in which the soul is implied:

> Mes yeux plongaient plus loin que le monde réel . . .
> Et les étoiles d'or, légions infinies,
> A voix haute, à voix basse, avec mille harmonies . . . ('Extase')

But another pattern is established from Keats, Shelley and Baudelaire, leading to the Symbolists. When we reach Keats, Shelley and Baudelaire, we detect a sudden emphasis of the olfactory sense and of taste in the language used to denote *soul*. Keats stresses the sense of taste:

> Now I have tasted her sweet soul to the core (*Endymion*)

Shelley offers us examples of the use of the olfactory sense:

> And in the soul a wild odour is felt (*Epipsychidion*)

In Baudelaire the olfactory is pervasive:

> Pendant que le parfum des verts tamariniers,
> Qui circule dans l'air et m'enfle la narine,
> Se mêle dans mon âme au chant des mariniers ('Parfum Exotique')

as well as the sense of taste:

> Elle se répand dans ma vie
> Comme un air imprégné de sel. ('Hymne')

In Verlaine the olfactory is again highlighted:

> De parfums lourds et chauds, dont le poison
>   Dahlia, lys, tulipe et renoncule
> Noyant mes sens, mon âme et ma raison
>   ('Crépuscule du Soir Mystique')

The course from exalted vision to sensual connotation typifies the soul's descent.

There are also examples conveying the physical imperfections of the soul which are a far cry from its perfectibility in Wordsworth. Pointing to these imperfections are qualifiers relating to its malleability such as in Jean-Paul's 'mollified soul':

> . . . der Gesang der Dichter und der Nachtigallen tiefer in die aufgeweichte Seele quillt (*Titan*)

The mollified soul is steeped deeper in the song of the poets and of the nightingales.

and Baudelaire's 'cracked bell' of a soul:

> Moi, mon âme est fêlée ('La Cloche Fêlée')

or Rimbaud's distortions which he calls monstrous:

Mais il s'agit de faire l'âme monstrueuse . . . ('Lettre au Voyant')

or the humid soul of Maeterlinck: 'âme humide' ('Ame Chaude') or the dampness in T. S. Eliot:

I am aware of the damp souls of housemaids
('Morning at the Window')

to name only a few.

If a texture is attributed to the soul by this steadily increasing sensuous vocabulary, a final mention should be made of other evidences of failure: language relating to erosion. Some instances occur as early as Hölderlin and Kleist. In Hölderlin we have noted the use of the word 'winden' (twist). In Kleist the word 'matt' (weary) appears. In Keats there are words such as 'entangle', 'trammel', 'enwrap', 'fatigue', 'ache', and twang'. In Baudelaire there is the word 'fêlé' (cracked). In Maeterlinck we note the words 'enclose' (enclosed), 'piège' (trap) and 'lasse' (tired). In T. S. Eliot we find the words 'stretched', 'misshapen', and 'lame'. The process of erosion has been occurring and through keywords the process is suggested; this is the final evidence of the transition from the spiritual to the sensual language in depicting the soul.

III RHETORICAL STRUCTURE

The fundamental rhetorical change suggestive of the shift in meaning of the soul is the transition from monologue to dialogue. In examples drawn from the first half of the century, the soul is isolated. Entire works centre upon the soul. The first person singular possessive adjective (my) is frequently used with the soul conveying an identity between the speaker and the spiritual principle in its integrity which the soul represents. In Wordsworth there is description of its ascension. In Lamartine there is meditation by the soul which infringes on the expressive ego. In Shelley the soul is evoked in the framework of the monologue: a single speaker in direct discourse.

Devices of personification and verbal interrogation occur from Baudelaire on. Indeed, one of the major structures which emerges reflecting the split between the self and the soul is the dialectic form, detected first in Baudelaire:

Et discutant avec mon âme déjà lasse ('Les Sept Vieillards')

Recueille-toi mon âme en ce grave moment,
Et ferme ton oreille à ce rugissement ('Le Crépuscule de Soir')

The second person plural pronoun 'toi' highlights the structure of exchange. The conversational medium is taken up by Verlaine:

Mon âme dit à mon coeur: Sais-je
Moi-même, que nous veut ce piège ('Ariettes Oubliées: vii')

The dialectic has also been located in two contemporaneous works: Richard Le Gallienne's 'The Decadent to his Soul' and Hofmannsthal's 'Psyche'. In Le Gallienne's poem, language with moralistic connotation describes the juxtaposition of soul and body. In 'Psyche' the dialogue takes the form of an argument. Active discourses between the soul and the self are presented, particularly pointing to the intransigence of the soul against the self's attempts at persuasion. The interchange reveals opposing personalities: the persuasive tone of the self's address is pitched against the curt and negative character of the soul's reply. In both instances the dialectics serve to undermine the soul.

It is in this light that one can observe the two distinct personae in Yeats' 'A Dialogue of Self and Soul' (1933), which will be analysed in terms of philosophical content in the final chapter. What is relevant to this discussion is form. The conversation is marked by aggressive rather than protective language. The self takes on authority on an equal footing with the soul. Interestingly, where Part i highlights the exchange, Part ii is a monologue of self because the soul has disappeared as a contender. The self and soul are at odds and although they use the dialogue form they are not communicating: they have no common ground for exchange. Whereas the self employs concrete language, the soul uses abstractions. When in the second part the responses of the soul are silenced, the self uses language that conciliates the concrete and the abstract. It incorporates the language of the soul into the dimension of the earthly self.

The shift, then, from meditation to conversation is a structural parallel between the previous unity of the soul and its final polarization. The ineffectiveness of the dialectics silences the conversation. And when the intimate rapport is disrupted the self appears to have rejected the soul as if it were foreign to its nature.

The personal lyricism of the early Wordsworth, characterized by direct evocation of a soul which is inseparable from the speaker, is thus gradually transformed. When the soul is the ingredient of the subjective, it cannot be separated to be perceived as an object. Rather, it is conveyed directly in the language identifying the speaker, the poet, with the inner being which he conveys in descriptive language, effusive and circumlocuting the essence or soul. The typical Romantic is intent on its most direct expression. The lyricism decreases, however, as the objectification of the soul augments. Gradually, the soul, through image, metaphor and metonymy becomes symbol and the target of indirect expression of subjectivity. While it is symbol it is suggestive of the state of the subject. When it finally becomes persona in dialogue, it has an existence of its own, independent and even antithetical to the writer who created the dialogue.

8   The Philosophical Evolution

The metaphoric transformation that we have observed in the poetry of the nineteenth century is not merely a stylistic effect. It is symptomatic and illustrative of a philosophical evolution affecting philosophers and poet-philosophers alike. Our study has heretofore dealt primarily with poetic metaphor. But this does not mean that the phenomenon observed relates merely to a small sector of poets. We are supported, rather, by the philosophical statements in pure philosophy as well as in literary prose writings having contiguity with the poetic writings previously examined. In fact Jung, looking back on nineteenth-century philosophic thought, focuses on this transformation of the notion of soul as a momentous factor which he calls 'the psychology of soullessness':

> Nachdem das Mittelalter sowohl wie die Antike, ja sogar die ganze Menscheit seit ihren ersten Anfängen von der Uberzeugung einer substanziellen Seele ausgegangen war, enstand in der zweiten Hälfte des 19. Jahrhunderts eine Psychologie 'ohne Seele'.[1]

> From the time of the Middle Ages as well as from that of Antiquity, moreover, since its foremost beginnings the whole of humanity had proceeded from the conviction of a substantial soul: there emerged in the second half of the nineteenth century a psychology of 'soullessness'.

The synthesis which these additional evidences make possible demonstartes the extensive and persuasive character of this changing vision of the soul-factor.

In returning to the early part of the nineteenth century, we are confronted with the transcendental movement and its parallel attitude in the prose writings of Coleridge,[2] and find in them a more direct treatment of what we have discovered as the dualistic identification of the soul and have discussed in terms of poetic metaphor. Though the language is more abstract, the vision is similar.

It is obvious to see in reading Coleridge's major philosophical work, *Aids to Reflection* (1825) that in line with his generation he takes the existence of the 'immortal soul' for granted. However, influenced as he is by the German philosophers, he leans heavily upon the Fichtean principle of self-reflection[3] and makes self-consciousness the 'key to the casket'[4] in the search for spiritual truth. Coleridge is able to conciliate the immortal character of the soul with the physical reality of the being who takes possession of the notion of immortality. He splits the spiritual element into two; the one, the over-soul, a universal, englobing, and remote presence, transcending human accessibility, and the other inhabiting and comprehensive of the self. It is both transcendent and immanent, universal and individual. In this perspective it is the eye that assumes the position of perception of the inner identity of the life-soul and the premonition of the macrocosmic and metaphysic presence of the universal soul beyond:

> Life is the one universal soul, which by virtue of the enlivening Breath, and the informing Word, all organized bodies have in common, each after its kind. This, therefore, all animals possess, and man as an animal. But, in addition to this, God transfused into a man a higher gift, and specially imbreathed; – even a living (that is, self-subsisting) soul, a soul having a life in itself. 'And man became a living soul.' He did not merely possess it, he became it. It was his proper being, his truest self, the man in the man ... Nothing is wanted but the eye, which is the light of this house, the light which is the eye of this soul. This seeing light, this enlightening eye, is reflection.[5]

This is a view which is to be particularly adopted by the group in America known as Transcendentalists. For instance in a passage from Emerson where the word *soul* is not even mentioned, we know that he is grasping both its centre and inner presence with what he calls 'the transparent eyeball':

> I become a transparent eyeball; I am nothing; I see all; the currents of the Universal Being circulate through me; I am part or parcel of God.[6]

On the other hand, he takes the special understanding of self observed in Coleridge and calls it the 'aboriginal Self' which in turn incorporates many of the elements of soul:

> What is the aboriginal Self, on which a universal reliance may be grounded? What is the nature and power of that science-baffling star, without parallax, without calculable elements, which shoots a ray of beauty even into trivial and impure actions, if the least mark of independence appear? We denote this primary wisdom as Intuition, whilst all later teachings are tuitions. In that deep force, the last fact behind which analysis cannot go, all things find their common origin.[7]

In fact Emerson develops a creed in 'The Over-Soul' (1841) which emulates the doctrine of soul, both in its individual and universal connotation.

But Emerson does not stop with the eyes as the connecting link between inner soul and over-soul. His efforts to bridge the gap first crystallize in fluidity: an ethereal substance ('ethereal water'[8]) that like a river with an unseen source flows into him from points beyond. Finally he completely eliminates the notion of substance and identifies the dual reality of the soul as a force, an energy, at once luminous, transparent and penetrating. It is obvious that Emerson's successive efforts to define soul in terms of position, form, and quality convey an uncertain but decidedly positive presence, hauntingly ever-present in his ontological as well as literary orientation. His view that the past offers inadequate delimitations of soul leads him to attempt a series of approximations of the soul element:

> All goes to show that the soul in man is not an organ, but animates and exercises all the organs; is not a function, like the power of memory, of calculation, of comparison, but uses these as hands and feet; is not a faculty, but a light; is not the intellect or the will, but the master of the intellect and the will; is the background of our being, in which they lie – an immensity not possessed and that cannot be possessed. From within or from behind, a light shines through us upon things and makes us aware that we are nothing, but the light is all.[9]

What emerges is not a definition of soul but an argument for its presence.

What makes Emerson so concerned with human conduct is the firm conviction that there is a bridge and a connection, an eventual transcendence of the human to join the immortal. Therefore his images of man are not merely flooded with heavenly lights; the metaphysical concerns determine the moral postures as well as the aesthetic representations. What interests us here is the fact that beyond the moralistic meditations for which Emerson is best known looms the same ascending soul concept that we have viewed in the Romantic poets and their orientation in the great chain of being, though the notion is conveyed in more abstract form than in metaphor:

> The soul's advances are not made by gradation, such as can be represented by motion in a straight line, but rather by ascension of state, such as can be represented by metamorphosis – from the egg to the worm, from the worm to the fly.[10]

Another instance within the transcendental strain of the identification of the soul with the search for self is Thoreau's *Walden* (1854). The most striking aspect of his concern with soul is to be found in the chapter entitled 'Higher Laws'. There, the metaphoric pattern of hunting and fishing offers spiritual gains as its result, specifically in the form of selfhood. Thoreau likens the search for soul to the penetration of the forest and his approach, like Emerson's, is with the aboriginal, 'the most original part of himself'.

> Such is oftenest the young man's introduction to the forest, and the most original part of himself. He goes thither at first as a hunter and fisher, until at last, if he has the seeds of a better life in him, he distinguishes his proper objects, as a poet or naturalist it may be, and leaves the gun and fish-pole behind.[11]

Both in Emerson and in Thoreau we find the same need for a return to the primeval in the identification of the soul, as was the case in Wordsworth. But whereas the primal in Wordsworth was associated with childhood, in the new country it is associated with virgin forests and primitive landscapes.

We find that Walden is another englobing example of the expression of soul as moral and metaphysical essence captured in the course of self exploration. What we have noted here is the manifestation of an epistemology of self which bears upon an ontology of soul. As was true in Emerson so with Thoreau, those 'higher', spiritual laws of which he speaks relate to the full apprehension of the soul by the individual; and the moral conduct is furthered by Thoreau in view of the ultimate assessment of man as the immortal being.

The connection between inner soul-self and over-soul is not always as convincingly envisaged as in the above instances. Sometimes in transcendental thought the soul is distinctly absent from the worldly vision, is antithetical to physical nature, and relates exclusively to other-worldliness. Coleridge's distinction between 'Nature' and 'Spirit' in one of the most notable passages of his *Aids to Reflection* offers an example:

> I have attempted, then, to fix the proper meaning of the words, Nature and Spirit, the one being the antithesis to the other: so that the most general and negative definition of nature is whatever is not spirit; and vice versa of spirit, that which is not comprehended in nature; or in the language of our elder divines, that which transcends nature ... It follows, therefore, that whatever originates in its own acts, or in any sense contains in itself the cause of its own state, must be spiritual, and consequently supernatural.[12]

This other relationship between poetic and prose determination of the soul is their mutual orientation toward Swedenborgian philosophy. We find it here in Coleridge's view of nature as the correspondent of the spiritual world. It is to be transmitted to Carlyle in particular, crystallized in his 'clothes philosophy' which envisages the universe as the living emblem and garment of the supernatural. It receives priority in Emerson as well: 'Every natural fact is a symbol of some spiritual fact.'[13] This entire context emphasizes that essential dualism at the basis of the Romantic soul concept.

Another factor relating to soul identification which we find in Coleridge is that of substitution of an equivalent for soul: a practice which becomes appropriated by the philosophers. In Coleridge, the concept of mind contains properties of rational power on the one hand and 'reason' on the other. Where the former relates to the phenomenal world, the latter transcends that world to the spiritual beyond. 'Reason' as an implied substitute for soul is a pure quality closer to spirit and soul than to rational power. Proceeding from the Kantian distinction between 'reason' and 'understanding', Coleridge envisages the soul with the properties of the former:

> The reason, as the integral spirit of the regenerated man, reason substantiated with vital, 'one only', yet 'manifold, overseeing all, and going through all' understanding; the breath of the power of God, and a pure influence from the glory of the Almighty; which remaining in itself' regenerateth all other powers, 'and in all ages entering into holy souls maketh them friends of God and prophets . . .'[14]

In reading the Transcendentalists we find then a dual feature relating to preoccupations with the soul: on the one hand there is a suction of the outer spirit into earthly being, thereby creating a sense of unity between man and the beyond, on the other hand there is also the Swedenborgian concept of distance, correspondence, and aspiration. Both elements of transcendentalism were, as we have seen, equally manifest in Romantic poetry's structure of the soul metaphor.

Outside the transcendental context but still within the Romantic vein, other prose manifestations of a Romantic soul concept, offering new factors of 'ego-making', 'dream', and aestheticism are to be found representatively in three separate documents: Keats' journal letter to his brother of April 1819, Gotthilf Heinrich von Schubert's *Die Geschichte Der Seele* (1830), and Poe's 'The Poetic Principle' (1850). What ties these three seemingly disparate documents together is their introduction of a new frame of reference intimating significantly the *human* element of the soul's vacillation.

We note that Keats' 'principle of soul-making' readily associates the soul with the concept of the ego rather than with the other-wordly spirit and thereby stresses the human notion of identity rather than the supernatural one of divine spirit and essence:

> Call the world if you please 'the vale of Soul-making'. Then you will find out the use of the world . . . I say 'Soul-making'. Soul as distinguished from an Intelligence. There may be Intelligences or sparks of the divinity in millions but they are not souls till they acquire identities, till each one is personally itself.[15]

Here as in his poetry, Keats interprets the soul as a factor in the wordly vision and inseparable from physical process. It does not exist *a priori* in a transcendental world but rather is developed empirically through the physical world, acquiring identity and reaching the standard of perfection in 'the here and now' that is assigned by the Christian to the beyond. The poet brackets the question of immortality in order to attribute to the human soul the credit for an immortal status. Keats substitutes for the standard Christian notion of the immortality of the soul a notion closer to a mortal soul which is created and developed through the processes of life and in particular, for the poet, through the trials and tribulations of human suffering. The critic Claude Finney has used this reference to demonstrate the 'empirical psychology' and 'philosophic humanism' that he has discerned in the poet. Our interest in this passage is not the same as Finney's. What is to be noted in the context of this study is how the passage mirrors the poet's notion of soul and his aesthetics. The poet arrives at the process of soul-identification through the poetic work of art rather than by means of a preconceived theological notion and thus the aesthetic supersedes the abstract expression of the soul:

> This point I sincerely wish to consider because I think it is a grander system of salvation than the Christian religion – or rather it is a system of Spirit creation.[16]

A similar sense pervades Poe's approach to the transcendence of the soul in 'The Poetic Principle'. There the discussion is strikingly central to the poet's aesthetics. Like Keats, Poe associates the soul more specifically with the human element of creativity. The process by which the soul contacts the 'supernal' is marked by transiency, and the struggle to acquire permanency is characteristic of the creative act. Though the aspirations of the soul relate to the eternal sphere, its activity is firmly grounded in the earthly context of the human senses and sentiment. The thirst for the supernal beauty is testimony of the immortal impulse in an otherwise mortal being: 'It is the desire of the moth for the star.'[17] We notice that the substitution for soul in Poe is not in abstraction but in a concrete physical reality of the moth and the star. Why the conjunction of the moth and the star? First the moth is among the most menial and ephemeral of existences. But, second, it has the power of metamorphosis from something that creeps to something that has wings and flies toward the light. The star in all poetic writings from earliest times to the Romantics is the highest envisagement of the luminous, visible reality, but unreachable as well. The linking of the lowliest to the highest, and the most fragile to the most permanent brings to light that upward aspiration and longing, the desire and the promise of fulfilment although the distance between moth and star, poetically conceivable, is none the less physically unfeasible. Poe's image supports the concrete orientation with which Shelley and Keats viewed the soul in both its aspirations and its futility.

Gotthilf Heinrich von Schubert, the German Romantic philosophical essayist responsible for an entire treatise on the soul, *Die Geschichte der Seele*, conveys much of the typical Romantic view of the soul. Like the Transcendentalists, Schubert views the soul in its universal and individual connotation. He gives these two aspects of a soul a structure through the notion of a circuitous journey; the universal light setting forth from the eternal sphere, penetrating the human and contacting the divine within:

> Dieses Ausgehen der Seele, zuerst in den buntfarbigen Schein der Leiblichen Gestaltung, welche dass Leben nur sinnbildlich erfasset, dann in das Wesen des Menschen, wie endlich in diesem die Seele zu sich selber und zu Gott komme: dies zu beschreiben ist die Aufgabe und der Endzweck der Psychologie.[18]

> This emanation of the soul, first in the variegated shine of the bodily form, which life lays hold of only symbolically, then into the being of men where finally the soul reaches itself and God: to describe this is the task and ultimate object of psychology.

Though holding the strict dichotomy of soul and body, the anthropologically oriented philosopher tends toward an Aristotelian discussion of the soul's workings and traffic ('der Verkehr') with the body and views the soul in terms of the life breath permeating corporeity: 'der Lebenshauch der irdischen Leiblichkeit'.[19] And the one major factor which distinguishes his psychology from the general transcendental vision of soul is the element of the dream. The introduction of the unconscious as territory for the soul is decidedly new:

> Im Traume, wenn die Seele . . . vom Leibe etwas frei geworden . . .[20]

> In the dream when the soul . . . has become somewhat freed from the body . . .

The critic Béguin has detected the dream in Schubert and used it as a basis for linking Schubert with modern psychology. But more significant is the philosophic implication of the introduction of the new territory: the unconscious realm foreshadows the inclination toward a more human context of the soul despite the standard belief in its immortal nature and otherwordly affinities.

When we view the documents that are more strictly philosophical we find the approaches of Hegel and Schopenhauer to the problem of soul most appropriate to our study. We notice that their systems fail to offer the resort of transcendance of soul so prevalent in Transcendentalism and in the corresponding manifestations in early European Romanticism. The movement is away from the dualistic system posited by the philosophical structure upon which transcendentalism is built toward an evolving monistic trend which incorporates the soul into a larger notion of spirit.

Though Hegel's *Phänomenologie des Geistes* (1807), *Enzyklopädie der philosophischen Wissenschaften im Grundriss* containing *Die Philosophie des Geistes* (1917) and Schopenhauer's *Die Welt als Wille und Vorstellung* (1818) appeared during the period belonging to Romanticism, the perspective with which these works envisage soul relates more specifically to poetic writings dating from Baudelaire and the Symbolists. This is not surprising, since philosophy tends to forecast future trends in poetic sensibility.

The disruption of the soul on the philosophical level is particularly manifest in the identification of soul with notions of finitude (*Endlichkeit*), passivity (*Passivität*), potentiality (*Möglichkeit*), and sleep (*Schlaf*) most clearly spelt out in Hegel's sketch of the philosophical sciences in which soul occupies a primitive primal position in the scheme leading to actualization of Spirit:

> Sie ist die Substanz, die absolute Grundlage aller Besonderung und Vereinzelung des Geistes, so das er in ihr allen Stoff seiner Bestimmung hat, und sie die durchdringende, identische Idealität derselben bleibt.[21]

> It is the substance, the absolute foundation of all particularization and individualization of the spirit (Geist); the spirit has in it all the material of its determination, and the soul remains the penetrating, selfsame identity of it.

That soul is relegated to a position of sleep and potentiality emphasizes its inferior position in regard to the higher principle of 'Geist' which evolves and which is the crux of the Hegelian vision of reality. Its designation as a passive entity sets it apart from 'Geist' which is characterized by dynamism and activity:

> Nur die Seele ist passiv, – der freie Geist aber wesentlich activ, producirend.[22]

> Only the soul is passive, whereas the free spirit is by nature active and producing.

Untypical of the Romantics, Hegel makes a distinction between soul and spirit, granting a passive role to soul and an active one to spirit which becomes associated with a dynamic force.

The most obvious manner in which the notion of soul is changed, then, is in the priority given to the notion of 'Geist' and the implications of the term in the Hegelian scheme. 'Geist' is distinctly devoid of the religiosity associated with its English equivalent of 'spirit'. Nor does it bear the theological connotation that we sensed in Novalis' use of the word in his *Geistliche Lieder* noted earlier in this study. Instead, notions such as *Phänomenologie* (*Die Phänomenologie des Geistes*) and (*Wirklichkeit* ('die Wirklichkeit des Geistes'[23]) highlight the association of 'Geist' with worldly and human situations.

The interplay of 'Geist' and world is particularly noted in the relationship established between 'Geist' and the principle of corporeity known as *Leiblichkeit*. The two notions are not diametrically opposed; rather *Leiblichkeit* is the actualization of 'Geist'.

That spirit is spoken of in terms of corporeity is particularly lucid in the section of *Die Philosophie des Geistes* devoted to the discussion of art. We have already discerned that Keats and Poe saw fit to view the soul at the centre of the creative act and as the focus of the earthly sensibility. We have noted their approach to the soul through aesthetics. Here in Hegel we find that art also is considered as one of the highest manifestations of his substitute for soul, 'Absolute Spirit'. In particular, classical art with its stress on the human body is the most vivid illustration that Hegel can offer of the interrelationship of spirit and corporeity:

> Unter den Gestaltungen ist die menschliche die höchste und wahrhafte, weil nur in ihr der Geist seine Leiblichkeit und hiermit anschaubaren Ausdruck haben kann.[24]

> Among forms, the human one is the highest and the true because only in it can the spirit have its corporeity and along with it its visible expression.

This stage in the philosophical evolution of the soul is particularly in line with the pagan notion of soul detected in the Romantics proceeding from Keats and Shelley in which the mingling of the material and the spiritual is most evident. Interestingly, the philosophical historian, Frederick Copleston, in the course of the explication of this aspect of Hegel's thought, alludes to the parallel in the craft of Praxiteles which is the classic symbol or the incorporation of the ineffable 'Spirit' into the tangible material form.[25] For a more contemporary adaptation of the Praxiteles reference, we can go to Hawthorne's *The Marble Faun* (1859), where Hawthorne refers to a sculptor who defined his own vision of the unity of spirit and matter in the embodiment of a statue of which he discerned the sacred character in this very union of the tangible, endurable material substance infused with the ephemeral spirit of human creativity:

> A sculptor, indeed, to meet the demands which our preconceptions make upon him, should be even more indispensably a poet than those who deal in measured verse and rhyme. His material, or instrument, which serves him in the stead of shifting and transitory language, is a pure, white, undecaying substance. It insures immortality to whatever is wrought in it, and therefore makes it a religious obligation to

commit no idea to its mighty guardianship, save such as it may repay the marble for its faithful care, its incorruptible fidelity, by warming it with an ethereal life. Under this aspect marble assumes a sacred character; and no man should dare to touch it unless he feels within himself a certain consecration and a priesthood, the only evidence of which, for the public eye, will be the high treatment of heroic subjects, or the delicate evolution of spiritual through material beauty.[26]

If one were to speak for the place of soul and spirit in the scheme above, it would be clear that soul would be equated with the Aristotelian notion of substantial reality whose monistic basis posits substratum as inseparable from the formal principle of creative energy, here in terms of 'Geist'. The marble work of art is the most vivid metaphor of the compounding of soul into spirit.

This is indeed very representative of that stage in the evolution of the soul image beyond the initial systematic duality conceived by the typical Romantic and before the total reduction of the soul concept to material dimensions. For this very reason Hegel, though contemporary with the Romantic era, cannot be said to have unravelled a philosophy sustaining the Romantic mode. He can be said rather to have projected a modified concept of soul and to have created the nucleus of future accommodations to the ever rising materialism of the nineteenth century.

Where in Hegel the term 'soul' is compounded by the introduction of the term *Geist*, in Schopenhauer there is an outright dismissal of the word in its metaphysical sense. The word is only used in its metaphorical sense:

> Hingegen schon die Benennung 'Weltseele', wodurch Manche jenes innere Wesen bezeichnet haben, giebt statt desselben ein blosses ens rationis: denn 'Seele' besagt eine individuelle Einheit des Bewusseins, die offenbar jenem Wesen nicht zukommt, und überhaupt ist der Begriff 'Seele', weil er Erkennen und Wollen in unzertrennlicher Verbindung und dabei doch unabhängig vom animalischen Organismus hypostasirt, nicht zu gebrauchen. Das Wort sollte nie anders als in tropischer Bedeutung angewendst werden: denn es ist keineswegs so unverfänglich, wie ψυχή oder anima, als welche Athem bedeuten.[27]

However the expression 'world-soul', through which many have designated the inner being, denotes instead of that very being a bare *ens rationis*: for 'soul' signifies an individual unity of consciousness which actually does not befit that being, and on the whole the concept 'soul' is good for nothing since it hypothesizes knowledge and volition in inseparable union yet independent of the animal organism. The word should be used in no other than a figurative sense; for it is in no way as harmless as when like ψυχή or 'anima' it means breath.

In divesting the soul of its metaphysical signification, Schopenhauer only salvages its original designation of *anima* or breath which appears to be magnified into the central notion of Schopenhauer's thought: the force, energy or *Wille zum Leben*.

The introduction of the word concept of *Wille zum Leben* has significant implication in the transformation of the soul concept. In replacing the concept of soul as the keynote of being, 'will' becomes effectively associated with matter and the worldly context. The phenomenological viewpoint is at the forefront as the 'will' or active principle of energy inseparable from matter or its visible manifestation.

In the focus on empirical reality and the incorporation of the 'will' therein, what is to become closely associated with the phenomenological movement at the end of the century, the notion of *dasein*, begins to emerge, replacing *sein* and its affinity with a transcendental soul.

We find the notion of soul being drawn into this worldly context. The shift to worldliness is made especially manifest in Schopenhauer's discussion of death and its relation to the notion of 'will'. That the promise of an 'other-worldly' territory for the soul has been rejected is apparent in the concrete reference to a death sentence which fails to include an accompanying doctrine of immortality, as was true of the Platonic metaphor drawn from the *Phaedo* and discussed at the outset of this study. It is clear that the Platonic argument considers the stoic acceptance of death as the attitude most commensurate with the belief in the immortality of the soul. Here in Schopenhauer attention is drawn to the *angst* before death because of the disbelief in that immortality of soul. Death is the negation rather than the affirmation of that life principle, here known as 'will'. For the philosopher, the *angst* before death and the distaste of man before an execution is evidence that the notion of the *Wille zum Leben* as the principle of Reality grounded in the worldly domain has altered the notion of soul:

> Man sehe z.B. die unglaubliche Angst eines Menschen in Lebensgefahr, die schnelle und so ernstliche Theilnahme jedes Zeugen derselben und den gränzen-Jubel nach der Rettung. Man sehe des starre Entsetzen, mit welchem ein Todesurtheil vernommen wird, das tiefe Grausen, mit welchem wir die Anstalten zu dessen Vollziehung erblicken, und das herzzerreissende Mitleid, welches uns bei dieser selbst ergreift ... An solchen Erscheinungen also sichtbar, das ich mit Recht als das nicht weiter Erklärliche, sondern jeder Erklärung zum Grunde zu Legende, den Willen zum Legen gesetz habe, und das dieser weit entfernt, wie das Absolutum, das Unendliche, die Idee und ähnliche Ausdrücke mehr, ein leerer Wortschall zu sein, das Allerrealste ist, was wir kennen, ja, der Kern der Realität selbst.[28]

One sees for example the unbelievable anxiety of a man in mortal danger, the swift and earnest concern of every witness of it and the boundless joy after deliverance from it. One sees the motionless terror with which a death sentence is heard, the deep dread with which we view the preparations for its execution and the heartrending pity which lays hold of us in its midst ... In respect to such phenomena then, it becomes evident that I have reason to assert that the Will to Live is that which receives no further explanation but rather lies at the foundation of every explanation, and that far removed from the empty verbiage such as the absolute, the eternal, the Idea and other similar expressions, it is the most real thing that we know, truly, the kernel of reality itself.

Terms such as 'das Absolutum', and 'das Unendliche' which conjure soul and immortality are replaced by what the philosopher introduces as 'will' or the concrete manifestation of reality.

Indeed, with Schopenhauer and with Hegel we notice the beginning of a trend in philosophy to circumvent the word-concept 'soul'. In the era of Positivism, social philosophers like Taine and Mill exemplify this tendency. The words 'mind', 'intellect', 'ego', and 'self' assume growing significance and become increasingly confusing in the linguistic exchanges and equivalences when we conduct the discussion via translation. In a work such as Taine's *De L'Intelligence* (1870) we note that soul is considered as a metaphysical phantom, surviving in the form of a past signifier and is replaced by the new concept of interior being, 'le moi' or ego:

Car il ne s'agit plus de savoir comment une substance inétendue, appelée âme, peut résider dans une substance étendue, appelée corps, ni comment deux êtres de nature aussi différents peuvent avoir commerce entre eux; ces questions scolastiques tombent avec les entités scolastiques qui les suggèrent. Nous n'avons plus devant les yeux qu'une série d'événements appelée moi, liée à d'autres qui sont sa condition.[29]

Indeed it is no longer a question of knowing how an unextended substance called 'soul' can reside in an extended substance called 'body', nor how two entities as different as they are from each other can deal with each other; these scholastic questions are dropped along with those scholastics who suggest them. We have nothing more before our eyes than a series of events called 'self', bound to others which constitute its condition.

Of course the cause of the multiple substitutions to avoid the use of the word 'soul' is the new scientific orientation which contributes to the philosophical dismissal of soul as an unacceptable factor in a system of definition which accepts only material bases for both function and form.

The debate of soul versus body is no longer tenable and the function attributed to the soul now passes into the distinctions suddenly created by words that are originally synonymic. The soul factor has to be situated semantically since it no longer has an ontological validity. Mill's *Analysis of the Phenomena of the Human Mind* (1869) is significant precisely for the marked absence of the soul in a discussion which taking the soul's elimination for granted, focuses upon the mind and its phenomena:

> Philosophical inquiries into the human mind have for their main and ultimate object, the exposition of its more complex phenomena.[30]

A contemporary 'aesthetic' document which captures the new attention given to the self distinct from the purely Romantic spiritual subjectivity is Rimbaud's notable *Lettre à Paul Demeny* of 15 May 1871. There the French poet dismisses the traditional importance of *ego* and attributes a new connotation of *self* in terms of a drastically altered concept of soul. Rimbaud believes that the substance with which the poet works is a 'monstrous' soul. To cultivate this soul implies that the poet subject it to torture and dismemberment, submitting it to all the pains of the human, earthly body:

> Mais il s'agit de faire l'âme monstrueuse: à l'instar des comprachicos, quoi! Imaginez un homme s'implantant et se cultivant des verrures sur le visage.

Although we have referred to this quotation earlier in this study for its metaphoric signification, here we view it for its conceptual content. The monstrous soul, subjectivity made objective, is fully qualified by the element of corporeity. And designating it as such, the poet-seer foresees an increasingly materialistic future.

In the search for terms to replace the waning notion of soul it is ultimately in Nietzsche that we find a new importance attached to the concept of *selbst* or self closely akin to body and envisaged in the context of 'this world'. Interestingly, at this point the emphasis is upon the body, the incarnation of the worldly self, as the bridge to the 'here and now' or 'hic et nunc'; it replaces the transcendental vision of soul as the means to the hereafter.

In a section of *Also Sprach Zarathustra* (1883) entitled 'Von den Verächtern des Leibes' ('On the Despisers of the Body') in which the philosopher conveys his customary disdain for those who fail to rise to the level of the 'Übermensch', we find an array of words and concepts which are antithetical to soul and fill the void created by its elimination. The standard discussion of soul and body:

> Leib bin ich und Seele – so redet das Kind
>
> Body am I and soul – so speaks the child

is rejected for a series of substitutions of the soul:

> Aber der Erwachte, der Wissende sagt: *Leib* bin ich ganz und gar, und nichts ausserdem: und Seele ist nur ein Wort für ein Etwas am Leibe.
>
> Der Leib is eine grosse *Vernunft*, eine Vielheit mit einem Sinne...
>
> Werkzeug deines Leibes ist auch deine kleine Vernunft, mein Bruder, die du '*Geist*' nennst, ein kleines Werk und Spielzeug deiner grossen Vernunft.
>
> '*Ich*' sagst du und bist stolz auf dies Wort. Aber das Grossere ist, woran du nicht glauben willst – dein Leib und seine grosse Vernunft; die sagt nicht Ich, aber tut Ich...
>
> Werk und Spielzeuge sind *Sinn* und *Geist*: hinter ihnen liegt noch das *Selbst*.[31]

> But the Awakened One, the Knowledgeable One says: body (*Leib*) am I entirely and nothing besides; and soul (Seele) is only a word for something in the body.
>
> The body is a big Reason (*Vernunft*), a multiplicity with one meaning...
>
> The instrument of your body is likewise your little Reason, my brother, which you call 'Spirit' (*Geist*), a litle tool and toy of your big Reason.
>
> 'I' (*Ich*) you say, and are proud of this word. But the Bigger One, in which you don't want to believe, is your body and its big Reason; which does not say 'I' but does 'I'...
>
> Tools and Toys are mind (*Sinn*) and spirit (*Geist*); behind them lies yet the self (*Selbst*).

The imperial 'Selbst' (self) is commensurate with 'Leib' (body) and 'Geist' (spirit), prompting the movements of the phenomenal ego or 'ich'. Interestingly, the adjective 'schaffend' has been dislocated as well, relinquishing its function of defining the soul. Instead it qualifies both the self and the body, which have become, like the 'will' in Schopenhauer, substitutes for the soul.

But Nietzsche himself views this change as a transformation of the soul factor rather than its dismissal so as not to be vulnerable to the charges of nihilism. This attitude is made clear in a section of *Jenseits von Gut und Böse* (*Beyond Good and Evil*) (1886) which verbalizes the process that we have been studying in the course of our literary exploration. It is the most supportive statement of the identification of the soul with mortality:

> Es ist, unter uns gesagt ganz und gar nicht nötig, 'die Seele' selbst dabei loszuwerden und auf eine der altesten und ehrwürdigsten Hypothesen Verzicht zu leisten: wie est dem Ungeschick der Naturalisten zu begagnen pflegt, welche, kaum das sie an 'die

Seele' rühren, sie auch verlieren. Aber der Weg zu neuen Fassungen und Verfeinerungen der Seelen-Hypothese steht offen: und Begriffe wie 'sterbliche Seele' und 'Seele als Subjekts-Vielheit' und 'Seele als Gesellschaftsbau der Triebe und Affekte' wollen fürdenhin in der Wissenschaft Bürgerrecht haben.[32]

Between ourselves, it is not at all necessary, thereupon, for the soul itself to be dismissed and for one of the oldest and more respected hypotheses to be renounced as is usually the case of crude Naturalists who no sooner touch upon the soul but lose it. The way yet to a new version and refinement of the 'Soul-Hypothesis' stands open, and concepts such as 'mortal soul' and 'soul as subjective-multiplicity' and 'soul as complex of drives and passions' want henceforth to have citizenship in the city of science.

Unwilling to submit to the claims of the naturalist who in dismissing the soul factor transfers equal significance to a material factor, Nietzsche accords the soul an activity confined to its materialistic habitat. In so doing he offers a redefinition of soul. He attributes to soul a network of affections and forces of physical dimensions, introducing the way for a psychology which lacks the recourse to a metaphysical force implied in the old concept of soul. What is interesting here, however, is that in rejecting the form and function of soul, Nietzsche urges that the word itself and its ontological presence in the considerations of philosophy be retained.

This study of the metaphoric modification of the soul, though purely literary, has none the less vast implications in terms of the classification of literature. We are led to the conclusion that it is a misconception to view the movement from Romanticism to Symbolism as a continuation of the same lyricism and vision. Such a view falsifies the essence of the two literary movements. They are indeed diametrically opposed and function in separate spheres. The one, grounded as it is in duality, manipulates the soul concept as the bridge between two worlds. The other has forsaken other-worldliness and uses the soul concept as a signifier devoid of its original significance but becoming a temporary substitute for the new definition of human sensibility. The Romantic, realizing the fragmentary character of each of the five senses, seeks their unification through the poetic metaphor using the soul phenomenon as the integrating element. He turns to the concept of soul which includes but also ultimately transcends the physical structure. The poets of the latter half of the nineteenth century first seek this same unity in technical synaesthesia. When that device fails or becomes too mechanical the poetic camera focuses on a more permanent substitution of soul. Mortal soul or human soul are but the initial trials of what in the twentieth century we have come to know as man's *search* for the soul.

For a classic example of redefinition of the soul in the twentieth century, we can turn to Paul Valéry's *L'Ame et la Danse* (1921) which departs radically from the dialectical solutions anticipated of Socratic dialogue. This intellectual poet distorts both the form and function of the dialogue to destroy the former meaning of soul. In lieu of an omniscient Socrates we find a sage who is somewhat uncertain as to the definition of the concept in question, and it is the comrade Phaedrus who first points to phenomena which are descriptive of soul:

> Je rêve à ces contacts inexprimables qui se produisent dans l'âme entre les temps, entre les blancheurs et les passes de ces membres en mesure, et les accents de cette sourde symphonie sur laquelle toutes choses semblent peintes et portées . . . [33]

> I dream of these inexpressible contacts which are produced in the soul, between time lapses, the whiteness and the regular passage of these limbs, and the stresses of this muted symphony upon which all things seem fashioned and measured.

It becomes clear in the course of this discourse how closely identified the soul has become with the subconscious and how it has assumed therewith the position of a threshold between life and death.

The dialogue itself is set in a banquet scene and the discussion of the three speakers, Socrates, his comrade Phaedrus and the physician Eryximachus, stems from their reactions to the extravagant display of food and dancing before them. Whereas the physician longs for spiritual substitutes for the material excess, Socrates applauds the actions of the bodies which nourish themselves and more significantly of those which fluctuate in dance. He argues that the physiological functions therein displayed are the bases for the complex of affections and thoughts to which Eryximachus is alluding.

For Valéry, who had insisted upon the interface of poetry and philosophy, the metonyny around which the new definition of soul is construed is the dance. Other writings of his refer explicitly to a dance philosophy which mirrors the poet's aesthetics.[34] Here the dialectics of the dance pervade the dialogue, as the characters converse over that physiological phenomenon of dance which increasingly absorbs their attention. In observing the various aspects of the dancer Athikte, the conversant company participate in the psychic forces which compose the psychic event exteriorized. The body language of the dancer becomes a hieroglyphic for the phenomenon of the soul whose physical basis is accentuated and which is a function of movement. Intently they watch the scintillations of the dancer who destroys the validity of a dichotomous significance of mortality and immortality in claiming that she is neither dead nor alive. The dance which she perpetuates and whose significance the personae probe bears the attributes of perpetual movement, characterized by an uncanny voluptuousness and frenzied ecstasy. Motifs of bees, salamanders, and flames are descriptive of the movements which are self-perpetuating. The basis of the activity is the body whose actions constitute the dance. The soul, in effect has surrendered to the body.

Appropriately then it is the physician rather than the metaphysician who has the terms for a redefinition of soul. The tables are turned. And when traditionally questions for palliatives against the ennui of existence would be expected to be directed to a Socrates, here they are asked of a physician whose answers demolish the soul most blatantly:

> L'âme s'apparaît à elle-même, comme une forme vide et mesurable.[35]

> The soul is made manifest to itself as an empty and measurable form.

In accepting the condition of emptiness which the soul has assumed, the body transcends the soul. The terminology used is so concrete that there is reference to the lymph as the colourless substance, predominant in soul, which divests the body of the blood constituting its force and ecstasy. The panacea against the dead state of soul is the body whose movements of dance serve to emphasize that dance and dancer, movement and physical being are not to be distinguished.

We find Socrates ironically trying to reconcile himself to the new connotations of body and soul by subsequently thinking of the body in terms of the soul only to destroy the latter in so doing. He admits to the fact that the body is not an extended substance, but first rationalizes that the body wants to acquire the qualities of soul:

> Et le corps qui est ce qui est, le voici qu'il ne peut plus se contenir dans l'étendue! – Où se mettre? Où devenir? – Cet *Un* veut jouer à *Tout*. Il veut jouer à l'universalité de l'âme! Il veut remédier à son identité par le nombre de ses actes! Etant chose, il éclate en événements![36]

> And the body, which is what exists, can no longer contain itself within extended substance. Where to place it? Where to transpose it? This unity wants to take part in multiplicity. It wants to take part in the universality of the soul. It wants to restore its identity by the plurality of its acts. Being a thing, it bursts forth in movements.

But soon the soul is left behind when the body is clearly described as the seat of transcendence and the source of the supernatural. Philosopher Socrates who is customarily associated with promoting the soul, here is associated with the doctrine of body. And the language which is reminiscent of Platonic descriptions of the ecstasy of soul is now a signifier of the body.

The same Socrates who is admittedly baffled by the various facets of the dance before him, slowly arrives at its definition which in turn reflects the concept of body described above. The fundamental reality which Socrates himself admits to is the metamorphosis. The metonymy of the soul has reached its final phase in the attitude which Socrates takes. Just as the traditional Socrates is noted for his certitude in definition which corresponds in form to structures of permanence and stability, here his incertitude is the parallel in form of the subject matter: 'l'acte pur des métamorphoses'.[37]

When we confer with the poet-philosopher Yeats, we have already crossed that delicate threshold which opens new vistas, spheres, and ontological positions leaving the trailing visions of soul far behind. The schematic private iconography of a Yeats poem such as 'The Phases of the Moon' (1919) acquires universal significance in its graphic display of the displacement of the soul by the body. Such a transfer occurs midway in that particular lunar cycle charting the progress toward selfhood. For this poet the transformation of the soul into body is conveyed through an evolutionary process which ranks soul as the lowest order in the hierarchy leading to body. The poem isolates the critical moment, interpreted as an event, wherein the identity of the soul is lost and that of the body is asserted.

Whereas in earlier instances the waning of the soul was individualized, here the focus is upon the collectivity of that experience and its most total expression. Yeats' reference to the fact that 'Nietzsche is born' gives historical validity to the process described. And the historicity is heightened in drama: hence the description of the soul's futile struggle for self-preservation is comparable in intensity to the precarious position of Leda trying in vain to preserve her integrity in 'Leda and the Swan'. Fittingly, Yeats' own epistemological stand that the soul is no longer viable is expressed in a statement potent with Yeatsian metaphorical significance:

> The soul begins to tremble into stillness,
> To die into the labyrinth of itself![38]

The trembling of the soul unto stillness echoes suggestions of the muting effect in poets of the latter part of the nineteenth century. All discourse is lost as the soul is silenced unto eternity. And as it wanes into that stillness, it betrays its ontological identity, surrendering to the powers of the body with which it becomes incorporated. The act is dialectical; the image of the labyrinth conveys the intricacy of the matrix from which the new scheme arises.

The poem deals in abstractions, obsessively pitting the soul against the body as entities separate made single in the dialectical play:

> All thought becomes an image and the soul
> Becomes a body . . . [39]

Though the words of the speaker Robartes refer to Yeats' theory of art where the toil of thought is suddenly transformed into the perfection of art, and thought becomes form, they reflect in turn the priority given to body by investing it with that gift of art. The reveries of spirit removed from the natural world of matter are considered sterile and need to be fertilized. The sexual intimations intensify the physical import which the poet promotes. In evoking both the artist and the lover, Yeats offers two emblems relating directly to the bodily significance. The phases of the moon image suggest in *new* 'cradles' the beginning of another cycle through bareness and wasteland that restir the dichotomous significance despite the historical change that has assured the contrary.

Yeats' philosophical poem 'A Dialogue of Self and Soul' appears anticlimatic, only to reiterate a confrontation which has already been resolved. As victor (though debilitated as evidenced in the weariness of the body) the self is none the less willing to submit to the toils of earthly existence, which are its exigencies, and to assume the vulnerable human form. The creative element previously lodged in the soul cannot be separated from that form. Where earthly existence had been antithetical to the soul as witnessed in the Wordsworthian scheme charting the progress through the stages of man as being an anathema to the soul, here the references to those stages from boyhood to old age reveal that bodily activity is the requisite of selfhood. And Yeats features that selfhood emerging and shunning the tower of immobility.

The self rejects the still life that the soul offers, and in particular the imageless thought which 'scorns the earth'. It opts for the inconsistencies inherent in humanity, represented by 'unfinished man' whose destiny is to inherit the recurring vacillations descriptive of life.

In silencing the dialogue with the soul, the self appropriates a poetic monologue of Shakespearean temper, featuring quintessential man in the terms of a bodily self: awkward, clumsy, defiled; but esteemed not shunned. The self is rendered concrete through a persona who like Hamlet contemplates his precarious position in the throes of human existence and accepts it in its imperfections. It rejects lures of escapism and snares of dreams which a Romantic might have offered. It cultivates instead the intensity of the human experience replete with events and actions in which it knowingly participates. It follows such rhythms as war and love with a firm resignation and terminates its speech with words bearing the conviction of a creed which blesses the 'here and now', indifferent to the hereafter. We know very well that the bodily self has priority over the phantasmal soul, and Yeats seems to be pressing the point, perhaps to satisfy an obsession that still haunts him as a vestige of a past identification of sensibility.

The soul has set, and unlike the soul in Wordsworth's Ode, it fails to give hope of a future revival or rebirth. It is this spiritual problem of modern man which triggers the philosophical-psychologist Jung's search for the soul. As if the soul were a superstition, the new psychology steers clear of it, and finds substitution in the vast multifaceted territory of the self. The way has been paved for the phenomenology of the self. And in the distance, now foresaken, lies the transcendental soul.

Notes

Chapter 1

1. Plato, *Phaedo*, in *The Collected Dialogues*, ed. Edith Hamilton (New York: Bollingen Foundation, 1961) p. 63.
2. Ibid., p. 66.
3. Ibid., p. 43.
4. Ibid.
5. Aristotle, *De Anima*, trans. W. S. Hett (Cambridge, Mass.: Harvard University Press, 1936) p. 67.
6. Ibid., p. 69.
7. Ibid., p. 73.
8. St Augustine, *On Christian Doctrine*, trans. D. W. Robertson, Jr. (New York: Liberal Arts Press, Inc., 1958) p. 10.
9. Emanuel Swedenborg, *Heaven and Hell* (New York: Swedenborg Foundation, Inc., 1952) p. 50.
10. Ibid., p. 49.
11. Goethe, *Faust*, ed. Erich Trunz (Münich; C. H. Beck'sche Verlagsbuchhandlung, 1972), Part I, 'Vor dem Tor', p. 41.
12. See Gaston Bachelard, *La Psychanalyse du Feu* (Paris: Gallimard, 1965).
13. I. A. Richards, *The Philosophy of Rhetoric* (New York: Oxford University Press, 1936) p. 11.
14. C. M. Bowra, *The Romantic Imagination* (Cambridge, Mass.: Harvard University Press, 1957) p. 23.
15. Robert Langbaum, 'The Evolution of Soul in Wordsworth's Poetry', PMLA, LXXXII (1967).
16. See Robert Langbaum, *The Poetry of Experience* (New York: W. W. Norton & Company, 1957).
17. Langbaum, 'The Evolution . . .', p. 270.
18. Guy Michaud, *Message Poétique du Symbolisme* (Paris: Librairie Nizet, 1947) p. 266.
19. See M. H. Abrams, *The Mirror and the Lamp* (New York: W. W. Norton & Company, 1958) pp. 57–69.
20. Albert Béguin, *L'Ame Romantique et la Rêve* (Paris: Corti, 1939) p. 70.
21. Ibid., p. 398.
22. A. O. Lovejoy, *The Great Chain of Being* (Cambridge, Mass: Harvard University Press, 1936) p. 14.
23. F. O. Matthiessen, *American Renaissance* (London and New York: Oxford University Press, 1941), p. xv.
24. Carl Woodring, *Politics in English Romantic Poetry* (Cambridge, Mass.: Harvard University Press, 1970) p. 100.

Chapter 2

1. William Wordsworth, *Poetical Works*, ed. Thomas Hutchinson (London: Oxford University Press, 1969). When more than one reference is made to a

poem included in a collected edition, page and line reference will be shown in parentheses in the text.

2. See 'The World is too much with us . . .'

3. *The Prelude*, p. 521.

4. 'The Old Cumberland Beggar', p. 444.

5. Friedrich Hölderlin, *Hyperion: oder Der Eremit in Griechenland, Sämtliche Werke*, vol. 3, ed. Friedrich Beissner (Stuttgart, J. G. Cottasche Buchhandlung, 1958).

6. Hölderlin, *Der Tod des Empedokles, Sämtliche Werke*, vol. 4, ed. Freidrich Beissner (Stuttgart: J. G. Cottasche Buchhandlung, 1961).

7. Hölderlin, *Gedichte bis 1800, Sämtliche Werke*, vol. 1, ed. Friedrich Beissner (Stuttgart: J. G. Cottasche Buchhandlung, 1946) pp. 266–7.

8. Hölderlin, *Gedichte nach 1800, Sämtliche Werke*, vol. 2, ed. Friedrich Beissner (Stuttgart: J. G. Cottasche Buchhandlung, 1951) p. 75.

9. Ibid., p. 95.

10. Alphonse de Lamartine, *Méditations Poétiques* (Paris: Editions Garnier, 1950).

11. Joseph Freiherr von Eichendorff, *Werke und Schriften*, vol. 2 (Stuttgart: J. G. Cottasche Buchhandlung, 1940) p. 306.

12. Clemens Brentano, *Werke*, vol. 2 (Munich: Carl Hanser Verlag, 1963) p. 69.

13. Novalis, *Schriften*, vol. 1, ed. Paul Kluckhohn (Stuttgart: W. Kohlhammer Verlag, 1960).

14. Jean-Paul, *Werke*, vol. 3 (Munich: Carl Hanser Verlag, 1962).

15. Heinrich von Kleist, *Sämtlich Werke und Briefe*, vol. 1 (Münich: Carl Hanser Verlag, 1965).

16. Samuel Taylor Coleridge, *The Poems*, ed. Ernest Hartley Coleridge (London: Oxford University Press, 1960).

Chapter 3

1. My definition of the word 'human' is according to the definition given by Plato, to which reference was made earlier.

2. See, for example, Carlos Baker's *Shelley's Major Poetry* (New York: Russell & Russell, 1961) and Claude Finney's *The Evolution of Keats' Poetry* (New York: Russell & Russell, 1963) which are concerned with the philosophical and psychological content of the poets' poetry.

3. This information is gleaned from Murry's *Keats* (New York: Noonday Press, 1955) p. 176.

4. Percy Bysshe Shelley, *The Complete Poetical Works*, ed. Thomas Hutchinson (London: Oxford University Press, 1905).

5. John Keats, *Poetical Works*, ed. H. W. Garrod (London: Oxford University Press, 1970).

6. My interest in this image is not ideological but linguistic, as an example of the kind of metaphor that Shelley uses. On the ideological plane, Neville Rogers, in his book *Shelley at Work*, shows the extent to which Shelley assimilated the Platonic character of Dante's and of Cavalcanti's poetry and wove it into this poem. The notion of a world soul is conveyed in the passage cited.

7. C. M. Bowra, *The Romantic Imagination* (Cambridge, Massachusetts: Harvard University Press, 1957) p. 111.

8. Ibid., p. 242.

9. See Northrop Frye, 'The Drunken Boat: The Revolutionary Element in Romanticism', *Romanticism Reconsidered*, ed. Northrop Frye (New York: Columbia University Press, 1963).

10. So suggestive of the soul was *Alastor* that it prompted Harold Hoffman to entitle his book on the poem *The Odyssey of the Soul* (New York: Columbia University Press, 1953). Hoffman concentrates on the imagery of the poem and does not discuss the usage of the key word.

11. W. B. Yeats, 'The Philosophy of Shelley's Poetry', in *Essays and Introductions* (New York: Macmillan Co., 1961) pp. 94–5.

12. See studies of synaesthesia which lie somewhat outside the focus of this essay: Richard H. Fogle, 'Synaesthetic Imagery in Keats', *Keats: A Collection of Critical Essays*, ed. Walter Jackson Bate (Englewood Cliffs, N. J.: Prentice Hall, 1964); Glenn O'Malley, *Shelley and Synesthesia* (Evanston: Northwestern University Press, 1964).

Chapter 4

1. Victor Hugo, *Les Contemplations*, ed. Léon Cellier (Paris: Editions Garniers Frères, 1969).

2. Charles Baudelaire, *Oeuvres Complètes*, Pléiade edition (Paris: Gallimard, 1954).

3. Victor Hugo, *Oeuvres Poétiques Complètes* (Montreal: Editions Bernard Valiquette, 1944) p. 115.

4. Arthur Rimbaud, Lettre à Paul Demény, 15 May 1871, *Oeuvres Complètes*, ed. Rolland de Renéville, Pléiade edition (Paris: Gallimard, 1951), p. 253.

5. It is to be observed, however, that 'mon âme' is not always the *alter ego*. One has to be careful because often it is an endearing manner of addressing the beloved. In the poem 'Une Charogne', for example, when the poet writes 'Rappelez-vous l'objet que nous vîmes, mon âme', he is referring to his loved one with whom he contemplates a carcass.

6. Gérard de Nerval, *Oeuvres Complètes*, ed. Albert Bèguin, Pléiade edition (Paris: Gallimard, 1960).

Chapter 5

1. My observations about the soul in the Symbolist context do not hold in Verlaine's poetry *Sagesse*, written at the time of his brief reconversion to Catholicism. As in Rossetti and other Pre-Raphaelites in England, Verlaine's poetry in this interval reflects the Christian concept of soul.

2. Guy Michaud, *Message Poétique du Symbolisme* (Paris: Librairie Nizet, 1947), vol. 1, p. 115. I do not agree with his denigrating remark about the Romantic soul.

3. Verlaine, *Oeuvres Poétiques Complètes*, Pléiade edition (Paris: Gallimard, 1948).

4. Verlaine, 'La Bonne Chanson: XVIII', p. 113.

5. See Verlaine, 'Les Ingénus'.

6. See Verlaine, 'Ariettes Oubliées: I', *Romances Sans Paroles*.

7. Mallarmé, *Oeuvres Complètes*, Pléiade edition (Paris: Gallimard, 1945).

8. Albert Samain, *Oeuvres*, vol. 1 (Chartres: Editions Garnier, Mercure de France, 1913).

9. Jean Moreas, *Premières Poésies* (Poitiers: Mercure de France, 1907) p. 39.

10. Stuart Merrill, *Poèmes* (Paris: Mercure de France, 1897).

11. Jules Laforgue, *Oeuvres Poétiques* (Paris: Editions Pierre Belfond, 1965).

12. Jean Lorrain, 'Comme un Lointain Etang', in *La Poésie Symboliste*, ed. Bernard Delvaille (Paris: Editions Seghers, 1971), p. 161.

13. Emile Verhaeren, 'Londres', in *La Poésie Symboliste*, pp. 144–5.

14. See Maurice Maeterlinck, *Morceaux Choisis* (Paris: Nelson Editeurs, n.d.).

15. Ibid., pp. 216–17.

16. Maeterlinck, *Serres Chaudes* (Bruxelles: Paul Lacomblez, 1895).

17. See Maeterlinck, 'Ame de Serre'.
18. See Maeterlinck, 'Après-midi'.
19. See Maeterlinck, 'Ame Chaude'.
20. Verlaine, 'L'Angoisse', *Poèmes Saturniens*, p. 49.
21. Mallarmé, 'L'Azur', p. 37.

Chapter 6

1. Richard Le Gallienne, *English Poems* (London: John Lane, 1912), p. 94.
2. Ibid.
3. William Butler Yeats, 'The Autumn of the Body', in *Essays and Introductions*, p. 190.
4. Ibid., pp. 192–3.
5. Stefan George, *Das Jahr der Seele* (Berlin: Georg Bondi, 1916).
6. Whereas the dead park was already evident in Verlaine, it was the setting for dead memories rather than for dead souls. See Verlaine's 'Colloque Sentimental'.
7. Hugo von Hofmannsthal. *Gedichte und Lyrische Dramen* (Stockholm: Bermann-Fischer Verlag, 1946).
8. Rainer Maria Rilke, 'Orpheus, Eurydike, Hermes', in *Sämtliche Werke*, vol. 1 (Frankfurt: Insel Verlag, 1955).
9. T. S. Eliot, *The Complete Poems and Plays* (London: Faber & Faber, 1969.)
10. See Elizabeth Drew, *T. S. Eliot: The Design of his Poetry* (New York: Charles Scribner's Sons, 1949) pp. 124–6. For an alternative interpretation, see George Williamson, *A Reader's Guide to T. S. Eliot*, second edition (New York: The Noonday Press, 1966) pp. 167–8.

Chapter 7

1. Tzvetan Todorov, *Poétique de la Prose* (Paris: Editions du Seuil, 1971) p. 13.
2. *Longinus on the Sublime*, trans. W. Hamilton Fyfe (Cambridge, Mass.: Harvard University Press, 1960) pp. 205–7.
3. R. A. Foakes, *The Romantic Assertion* (New Haven: Yale University Press, 1958) p. 58.
4. William Butler Yeats, *The Collected Poems* (London: Macmillan, 1971) p. 495.

Chapter 8

1. Carl Jung, 'Das Grundproblem der gegenwärtigen Psychologie', *Wirklichkeit der Seele* (Zurich: Rascher Verlag, 1947) p. 1.
2. Although we have detected in Coleridge's poetry a tendency which removes him from traditional Romantic poetry, we find that his philosophy is typical and even descriptive of the Romantic vein. This seems, however, to pose no problem since Coleridge is a complex personage, torn between philosophy and poetry. We might speculate that where philosophy took him to the past, poetry drew him to the future.
3. See Fichte's *Wissenschaftslehre* (1794). In focusing on the poetic quality of Coleridge's solipsism in this chapter, we tend to identify Coleridge more closely with the post-Kantians, Fichte, Schelling and Jacobi, than with Kant himself. This is a departure from the position held by Coleridgeans in general. Critics such as Thomas McFarland and Kathleen Coburn, for example, consider Coleridge closer to Kant than to Schelling and thus take the emphasis away from the soul-self relationship.
4. S. T. Coleridge, *Aids to Reflection*, in *The Complete Works*, vol. 1 (New York: Harper & Brothers, 1853) p. 116.

5. Ibid., pp. 119–20.
6. Ralph Waldo Emerson, 'Nature', in *Selected Writings*, Modern Library edition (New York: Random House, 1950) p. 6.
7. Emerson, 'Self Reliance', ibid., p. 155.
8. Emerson, 'The Over-Soul', ibid., p. 262.
9. Ibid., p. 263.
10. Ibid., p. 265.
11. Henry David Thoreau, *Walden*, Dolphin Books edition (New York: Doubleday & Co., 1960) p. 181.
12. Coleridge, p. 263.
13. Emerson, 'Nature', p. 15.
14. Coleridge, p. 461.
15. *The Letters of John Keats*, ed. Maurice Buxton Forman (London: Oxford University Press, 1952) pp. 334–5.
16. Ibid., p. 335.
17. Edgar Allan Poe, 'The Poetic Principle', in *Selected Poetry and Prose*, Modern Library edition (New York: Random House, 1951) p. 338.
18. Gotthilf Henrich von Schubert, *Die Geschichte der Seele* (Stuttgart: J. G. Cottasche Buchhandlung, 1877) vol. 1, p. 2.
19. Schubert, vol. 2, p. 103.
20. Ibid., p. 32.
21. Georg Friedrich Hegel, *Die Philosophie des Geistes* in *Sämtliche Werke* (Stuttgart: Fr Frommanns Verlag, 1929) vol. 10, pp. 52–3.
22. Ibid., p. 305.
23. Ibid., p. 447.
24. Ibid., p. 448.
25. Frederick Copleston, S. J., *A History of Philosophy*. Image Books edition New York: Doubleday & Co., 1963) vol. 7, part 1, pp. 277–8.
26. Nathaniel Hawthorne, *The Marble Faun, or the Romance of Monte Beni* (Boston: Houghton Mifflin & Co., 1900) p. 152.
27. Arthur Schopenhauer, *Die Welt als Wille und Vorstellung* in *Sämtliche Werke*, vol. 2 (Leipzig: Insel Verlag, 1910) p. 1107.
28. Ibid., p. 1109.
29. Hippolyte Taine, *De L'Intelligence*, vol. 1 (Paris: Librairie Hachette, 1906) p. 350.
30. John Stuart Mill, *Analysis of the Phenomena of the Human Mind* (London: Longman's Green Reader & Dyer, 1869) p. 1.
31. Friedrich Nietzsche, *Also Sprach Zarathustra* in *Werke*, vol. 2 (Munich: Carl Hanser Verlag, 1960) p. 300.
32. Nietzsche, *Jenseits von Gut und Böse*, ibid., p. 577.
33. Paul Valéry, *Oeuvres*, vol. 2, Pléiade edition (Paris: Gallimard, 1960) p. 154.
34. See Valéry's 'Philosophie de la Danse' in *Oeuvres*, vol. 1, Pléiade edition (Paris: Gallimard, 1957) pp. 1390–403.
35. Valéry, vol. 2, p. 168.
36. Ibid., pp. 171–2.
37. Ibid., p. 165.
38. Yeats, *The Collected Poems*, p. 185.
39. Ibid.

Bibliography

I PRIMARY SOURCES

An Anthology of Nineties Verse, compiled and edited by Alphonse James Albert Symons (London: E. Mathews & Marrot Ltd, 1928).

Aristotle, *De Anima*, trans. W. S. Hett (Cambridge, Mass.: Harvard University Press, 1936).

Baudelaire, Charles, *Oeuvres Complètes*, Pléiade edition (Paris: Gallimard, 1954).

Brentano, Clemens, *Werke*, vol. 2 (Munich: Carl Hanser Verlag, 1963).

Coleridge, Samuel Taylor, *Aids to Reflection, The Complete Works of Samuel Taylor Coleridge*, vol. 1 (New York: Harper & Brothers, 1853).

— *The Poems of Samuel Taylor Coleridge*, ed. Ernest Hartley Coleridge (London: Oxford University Press, 1960).

Eichendorff, Joseph Freiherr von, *Werke und Schriften*, vol. 1 (Stuttgart: J. G. Cottasche Buchhandlung, 1940).

Eliot, T. S., *The Complete Poems and Plays* (London: Faber & Faber, 1969).

Emerson, Ralph Waldo, *Selected Writings*, Modern Library edition (New York: Random House, 1950).

George, Stefan, *Hymnen, Pilgerfahrten, Algabal* (Berlin: Georg Bondi, 1918).

— *Das Jahr der Seele* (Berlin: Georg Bondi, 1916).

Goethe, J. W. von, *Faust*, ed. V. Erich Trunz (Munich: C. H. Beck'sche Verlagsbuchhandlung, 1972).

Hardenberg, Friedrich von (Novalis), *Schriften*, vol. 1, ed. Paul Kluckhohn (Stuttgart: W. Kohlhammer Verlag, 1960).

Hawthorne, Nathaniel, *The Marble Faun, or the Romance of Monte Beni* (Boston: Houghton Mifflin & Company, 1900).

Hegel, Georg Wilhelm Friedrich, *Die Phänomenologie des Geistes*, ed. D. Johann Schulze, *Werke*, vol. 2., 2nd ed. (Berlin: Duncker und Humbolt, 1841).

— *Die Philosophie des Geistes, Sämtliche Werke*, vol. 10 (Stuttgart: Fr. Frommanns Verlag, 1929).

Hofmannsthal, Hugo von, *Gedichte und Lyrische Dramen* (Stockholm: Bermann-Fischer Verlag, 1946).

Hölderlin, Friedrich, *Gedichte bis 1800, Sämtliche Werke*, vol. 1, ed. Friedrich Beissner (Stuttgart: J. G. Cottasche Buchhandlung, 1946).
— *Gedichte nach 1800, Sämtliche Werke*, vol. 2, ed. Friedrich Beissner (Stuttgart: J. G. Cottasche Buchhandlung, 1951).
— *Hyperion: oder Der Eremit in Griechenland, Sämtliche Werke*, vol. 3, ed. Friedrich Beissner, Kleine Stuttgarter Ausgabe (Stuttgart: J. G. Cottasche Buchhandlung, 1958).
— *Der Tod des Empedokles, Sämtliche Werke*, vol. 4, ed. Friedrich Beissner (Stuttgart: J. G. Cottasche Buchhandlung, 1961).
Hugo, Victor, *Les Contemplations*, ed. Léon Cellier (Paris: Garniers Frères, 1969).
— *Oeuvres Poétiques Complètes* (Montreal: Editions Bernard Valiguette, 1944).
Jung, Carl, 'Das Grundproblem der Gegenwärtigen Psychologie', *Psychologische Abhandlung*, vol. 4 (Zurich: Rascher & Cie. Verlag, 1934).
— 'Seelenprobleme der Gegenwart', *Psychologische Abhandlung*, vol. 3 (Zurich: Rascher & Cie. Verlag, 1946).
Keats, John, *The Letters of John Keats*, ed. Maurice Buxton Forman, 4th ed. (London: Oxford University Press, 1952).
— *Poetical Works*, ed. H. W. Garrod (London: Oxford University Press, 1970).
Kleist, Heinrich von, *Sämtliche Werke und Briefe*, vol. 1 (Munich: Carl Hanser Verlag, 1965).
Lamartine, Alphonse de, *Méditations Poétiques* (Paris: Editions Garniers, 1950).
Le Gallienne, Richard, *English Poems*, 5th ed. (New York: John Lane Company, 1912).
Longinus, *Longinus on the Sublime*, trans. W. Hamilton Fyfe (Cambridge, Mass.: Harvard University Press, 1960).
Maeterlinck, Maurice, *Morceaux Choisis* (Paris: Nelson, n.d.).
— *Serres Chaudes*, (Brussels: Paul Lacomblez, 1895).
Mallarmé, Stephane, *Oeuvres Complètes*, Pléiade edition (Paris: Gallimard, 1945).
Merrill, Stuart, *Poèmes: 1887–1897* (Paris: Mercure de France, 1897).
Mill, John Stuart, *Analysis of the Phenomena of the Human Mind* (London: Longman's Green Reader & Dyer, 1869).
Moreas, Jean, *Premières Poésies: 1883–1886* (Paris: Mercure de France, 1907).
Nerval, Gerard de, *Oeuvres*, Pléiade edition (Paris: Gallimard, 1960).
Nietzsche, Friedrich, *Werke*, vol. 2, ed. Karl Schlecta (Munich: Carl Hanser Verlag, 1960).
Plato, *Phaedo, Collected Dialogues*, ed. Edith Hamilton (New York: Billingen Foundation, 1961).
Poe, Edgar Allen, *Selected Poetry and Prose*, Modern Library edition (New York: Random House, 1951).

La Poésie Symboliste, ed. Paul Delvaille (Paris: Editions Seghers, 1971).

Poètes Belges d'Expression Française, ed. Pol de Mont, 2nd ed. (Almelo: W. Hilarius, 1899).

Richter, Jean-Paul, *Werke*, vol. 3 (Munich: Carl Hanser Verlag, 1961).

Rilke, Rainer Maria, *Sämtliche Werke*, vol. 1 (Frankfurt am Main: Insel Verlag, 1955).

Rimbaud, Arthur, *Oeuvres Complètes*, Pléiade edition (Paris: Gallimard, 1951).

St Augustine, *On Christian Doctrine*, trans. D. W. Robertson, Jr (New York: Liberal Arts Press, Inc., 1958).

Samain, Albert, *Oeuvres*, vols 1 and 2 (Paris: Mercure de France, 1912).

Schopenhauer, Arthur, *Die Welt als Wille und Vorstellung*, Parts 1 and 2, *Die Ergänzungen zu den vier Büchern des Ersten Bundes, Sämtliche Werke*, vols. 1 and 2 (Leipzig: Insel Verlag, 1910).

Schubert, Gotthilf Heinrich von, *Die Geschichte der Seele*, vols 1 and 2 (Stuttgart: J. G. Cottasche Buchhandlung, 1877–78).

Shelley, Percy Bysshe, *The Complete Poetical Works*, ed. Thomas Hutchinson (London: Oxford University Press, 1905).

Swedenborg, Emanuel, *Heaven and Its Wonders and Hell From Things Heard and Seen* (New York: Swedenborg Foundation, Inc., 1952).

Taine, Hippolyte, *De L'Intelligence*, vol. 1, 11th ed. (Paris: Librairie Hachette, 1906).

Thoreau, Henry David, *Walden*, Dolphin Books edition (New York: Doubleday & Company, 1960).

Valéry, Paul, *Oeuvres*, vols. 1 and 2, Pléiade edition (Paris: Gallimard, 1957, 1960).

Valéry, Paul, *Oeuvres* vols 1 and 2, Pléiade edition (Paris: Gallimard, Gallimard, 1948).

Wordsworth, William, *Poetical Works*, ed. Thomas Hutchinson, rev. Ernest de Selincourt (London: Oxford University Press, 1969).

Yeats, William Butler, *Collected Poems* (London: Macmillan, 1971).

— *Essays and Introductions* (New York: Macmillan, 1961).

II CRITICAL WORKS CONSULTED

Abrams, M. H. *The Mirror and the Lamp: Romantic Theory and the Critical Tradition* (New York: W. W. Norton & Company, Inc., 1958).

— *Natural Supernaturalism: Tradition and Revolution in Romantic Literature* (New York: W. W. Norton & Company, Inc., 1971).

Bachelard, Gaston, *La Psychanalyse du Feu*, Idées edition (Paris: Gallimard, 1965).

Baker, Carlos, *Shelley's Major Poetry: The Fabric of a Vision* (Princeton: Princeton University Press, 1948).

Balakian, Anna, *The Symbolist Movement: A Critical Appraisal.* (New York: Random House, 1967).

Barzun, Jacques, *Classic, Romantic and Modern,* Anchor Books edition (New York: Doubleday & Company, 1961).

Bate, Walter Jackson, ed., *Keats: A Collection of Critical Essays* (Englewood Cliffs, N.J.: Prentice Hall, 1964).

Beach, Joseph Warren, *The Concept of Nature in the Nineteenth Century English Poetry* (New York: Pageant Book Company, 1956).

Béguin, Albert, *L'Ame Romantique et le Rêve: Essai sur le Romantisme Allemand et la Poésie Française* (Paris: Librairie José Corti, 1939).

Bertocci, Angelo, *From Symbolism to Baudelaire* (Carbondale: Southern Illinois University Press, 1964).

Bloom, Harold, *The Visionary Company* (New York: Doubleday & Company, 1963).

Bowra, C. M., *The Heritage of Symbolism* (New York: St. Martin's Press, 1967).

— *The Romantic Imagination* (Cambridge, Mass.: Harvard University Press, 1957).

Burke, Kenneth, *A Grammar of Motives* (Cleveland and New York: World Publishing Company, 1962).

Copleston, Frederick, S. J., *A History of Philosophy,* vol. 7, part 1, Image Books edition (New York: Doubleday & Company, 1963).

Drew, Elizabeth, *T. S. Eliot: The Design of His Poetry* (New York: Charles Scribner's Sons, 1949).

Finney, Claude, *The Evolution of Keats' Poetry,* vols 1 and 2 (New York: Russell & Russell, 1963).

Foakes, R. A., *The Romantic Assertion* (New Haven: Yale University Press, 1958).

Frye, Northrop, ed., *Romanticism Reconsidered: Selected Papers from the English Institute* (New York: Columbia University Press, 1963).

Ghil, René, *Les Dates et les Oeuvres: Symbolisme et Poésie Scientifique,* 6th ed. (Paris: Editions G. Crès et Cie., 1923).

Gottschalk, Hans, *Das Mythische in der Dichtung Hölderlins* (Stuttgart: J. G. Cottasche Buchhandlung, 1943).

Havens, Raymond Dexler, *The Mind of a Poet,* vol. 1, *A Study of Wordsworth's Thought* (Baltimore: Johns Hopkins Press, 1941).

Hoffman, Harold, *The Odyssey of the Soul* (New York: Columbia University Press, 1953).

Langbaum, Robert, 'The Evolution of Soul in Wordsworth's Poetry', PMLA, LXXXII, ii (May 1967) 265–72.

— *The Poetry of Experience* (New York: W. W. Norton & Company, 1957).

Lovejoy, A. O., *The Great Chain of Being* (Cambridge, Mass., Harvard University Press, 1936).

Matthiessen, F. O., *American Renaissance* (London and New York: Oxford University Press, 1941).

McFarland, Thomas, *Coleridge and the Pantheist Tradition* (London: Oxford University Press, 1969).

Michaud, Guy, *Message Poétique du Symbolisme* (Paris: Librairie Nizet, 1947).

Monk, Samuel H., *The Sublime: A Study of Critical Theories in XVIII-Century England* (Ann Arbor: University of Michigan Press, 1960).

Morier, Henri, *Dictionnaire de Poétique et de Rhétorique* (Paris: Presses Universitaires de France, 1961).

Murry, John Middleton, *Keats*, 4th ed., rev. and enl. (New York: The Noonday Press, 1955).

O'Malley, Glen, *Shelley and Synesthesia* (Northwestern University Press, 1964).

Praz, Mario, *The Romantic Agony* (New York: World Publishing Company, 1956).

Poulet, Georges, *Etudes sur le Temps Humain* (Paris: Plon, 1950).

Preminger, Alex, ed., *Encyclopedia of Poetry and Poetics* (Princeton: Princeton University Press, 1965).

Richards, I. A., *Coleridge on Imagination* (Bloomington: Indiana University Press, 1960).

— *The Philosophy of Rhetoric* (New York: Oxford University Press, 1950).

Rogers, Nelville, *Shelley at Work: A Critical Inquiry* (Oxford: Clarendon Press, 1956).

Silz, Walter, *Early German Romanticism: Its Founders and Heinrich von Kleist* (Cambridge, Mass.: Harvard University Press, 1929).

Starkie, Enid, *Baudelaire* (New York: New Directions, 1958).

Symons, Arthur, *The Symbolist Movement in Literature* (New York: E. P. Dutton & Company, 1919).

Todorov, Tzvetan, *Poétique de la Prose* (Paris: Editions du Seuil, 1971).

Unterecker, John, *A Reader's Guide to W. B. Yeats* (New York: The Noonday Press, 1959).

Vordtriede, Werner, *Novalis und die französischen Symbolisten* (Stuttgart: W. Kolhammer Verlag, 1963).

Weber, Jean-Paul, *Genèse de l'Oeuvre Poétique* (Paris: Gallimard, 1960).

Williamson, George, *A Reader's Guide to T. S. Eliot*, 2nd ed. (New York: The Noonday Press, 1966).

Wilson, Edmund, *Axel's Castle* (New York: Charles Scribner's Sons, 1931).

Woodring, Carl, *Politics in English Romantic Poetry* (Cambridge, Mass.: Harvard University Press, 1970).

— *Wordsworth* Boston: Houghton Mifflin Company, 1965).

Index